A Basic Course in
Modern Kurmanji

Peter Pikkert

ALEV
BOOKS

ALEV
BOOKS

"Believe, Think, Act"

www.alevbooks.com

alevbooks@gmail.com

1st printing 1991
2nd printing 2010

Dedicated to those seeking the spiritual and social welfare of the Kurdish people.

P. Pikkert

Editor's Preface

OVER RECENT YEARS a number of requests for a "textbook of Kurdish" have been directed my way by various ones who for one reason or another wish to become conversant in that language. Many who have made that request were not at that time even aware that Kurdish exists in more than one form and could easily be guided to the *Kurdish Basic Course* by Abdulla and McCarus, the latter of whom was my professor at the University of Michigan. But those who specifically want to learn Kurmanji-Kurdish are not well served by that book, the difference between that dialect and Kurmanji-Kurdish being considerable.

Many who were aware of the *Zwanzig Lektionen für Deutsche* by Dr. Zaradachet Hajo, a volume that, with the very gracious permission and assistance of the author I have been revising, have asked me if I would translate that book into English. That request I have always declined on the basis that the twenty lessons compare Kurdish grammar to German grammar. If the German were simply translated into English, the comparisons to German grammar would be of little help to the English speaker who couldn't use the lessons in the original German.

Then in 1988, with the generous help of some colleagues, we offered a month-long introductory course on Kurmanji-Kurdish for a handful of English speakers who had approached us for help. In order to prepare the lectures for that course, we gleaned a great deal from non-English sources, especially from Dr. Hajo's *Zwanzig Lektionen für Deutsche* and from Bedir Khan and Lescot's *Grammair Kurde*, but also relied heavily on our own data, gleaned from thousands of hours spent speaking, hearing, reading and writing the language.

The lessons presumed a basic familiarity with language learning, as all participants were already at least bilingual, but did not presume a prior knowledge of technical linguistics. The material was presented on the basis of Kurdish grammatical structure, such that even the material we gleaned from the *Zwanzig Lektionen* was often, but not always, re-organized. We organized our material into approximately 40 lectures and accompanied them with excerizes that were to be done partly in class and partly as homework. In addition, the students participated daily in Total Physical Response (TPR) drills and regular visits with native speakers.

Peter Pikkert was one of the students at that course and later drafted the present volume on the basis of his notes from the course. It was through his initiative that the contents were organized into the present twelve lessons. I have had the privilege to work through the entire set of lessons twice to eliminate misunderstandings and typos, but have not yet had opportunity to give adequate attention to the pedagogical presentation. Presently, learning from these lessons can perhaps be compare to going on a picnic taking a lovely baked hen but forgetting to take knives, forks, plates and all the other usual accoutrements. There is a lot of meat, but for the most part, you have to gnaw it off the bone for yourself!

In other words, I am aware that the presentation of information in these lessons often comes too fast and in an order that is less than ideal. And the exercises that accompanied the original lectures are not yet available here, nor are, of course, the TPR drills and the visits with native speakers. That makes these lessons much less effective than the original course, but I hope that they are not entirely useless, even in this form.

We would like to caution you against using these lessons to the exclusion of interaction with native speakers. The lessons were never intended to be used that way and without the opportunity to hear Kurdish spoken by native speakers, and to interact with them in Kurdish, these lessons will not take you very far. But when you do compare these lessons to what you hear from your native-speaker friends please do not be alarmed at the divergences you find between their speech and what is in these lessons. Kurdish is rich in dialects and almost every village will have a few peculiarities of its own. Nevertheless, there is a "standard" Kurmaji that has been developed (and is still being refined) by Kurdish scholars publishing for Kurds over the past half century. These lessons present a rather conservative example of that "standard Kurmanji" which can be nicely supplemented by interaction with native-speakers from a wide variety of Kurmanji dialects.

On the other hand, there are "dialects of Kurdish" that are so divergent from the Kurmanji presented here that these lessons would not be particularly helpful to the learners thereof. For example, the dialects south of Rewanduz and Mosul in Iraq, or those south of Urmiya in Iran are so different from the Kurmanji presented in these lessons as to render the latter rather useless. And the so-called "Zaza dialects" are, technically speaking, not Kurdish at all, but seperate Iranian dialects that have been surrounded by Kurdish for many centuries. Do not be surprised if you find an occasional speaker of any of the above who refers to his own language as a kind of Kurmanji. That does not automatically mean that these lessons will help you to learn his dialect.

In the beginning it may be a bit awkward to discover how similar the "standard Kurmanji" of these lessons and the natural speech of your Kurdish friend may be. Just showing him the lessons could be enough, but only if the lessons really do reflect his speech AND he is able to read Kurdish. If he cannot read Kurdish, you will have to read it to him. And if you don't read it very well, he may not be able to understand you! Nevertheless, after an hour or so of experimenting, you will probably be able to tell whether you are interacting with someone whose dialect is similar enough to these lessons. Even if there are minor variations in pronounciation, grammatical endings and occasional vocabulary items, a speaker of Kurmanji will normally recognize and respond to 95% of what is contained in these lessons. If, with practise and patience, he still cannot agree with more than 80% of what is contained here, you may be interacting with someone whose dialect is so different as to render the lessons rather unhelpful.

One place to begin might be the personal pronouns and the verb "to be" (1.4 and 1.5) and then the oblique case personal pronouns (1.10). If your friend basically agrees with those pronouns and that conjugation, you are on your way. If he only recognizes the oblique case pronouns and not those in 1.4 (direct case), you are probably dealing with a dialect from too far south to get any use out of these lessons. If you have both cases of pronouns but the direct case first-person plural is something like /ma/ and the second-person plural /şima/ or /sima/, you are probably dealing with a Zaza dialect. In these cases you will either need to find another textbook or other friends.

If your friends come from the area of Maraş or Konya in Turkey, you will find these lessons of only limited usefulness. Through the dialects spoken in those areas represent a kind of Kurmanji, it is a rather more divergent kind than most and seems to have a greater proportion of Turkish loan words than elsewhere. More research in needed on those dialects.

We wish the users of the *Basic Course* every success in becoming fluent in Kurmanji-Kurdish and in developing important relationships with this proud and brave people. Few people have suffered more than the Kurds in the past century from exploitation, abuse and neglect by their neighbours and the world community. It is my prayer that even such a volume as this can contribute to greater understanding and mutual appreciation. Despite political assertions to the contrary, the student will discover that the Kurdish language is beautiful, systematic and rich. The speakers of the language deserve to be treated with respect and fairness.

Terry Todd, Herborn, 1991

Contents

Chapter 1

Simple Sentences, Case and Gender

1.1 - Alphabet

The Kurmanji alphabet has eight vowels and twentythree consonants. The vowels are approximately as follows:

a - as in "c<u>a</u>r" and "b<u>a</u>r".
e - as in "b<u>u</u>t" and "m<u>u</u>d".
ê - as in "h<u>ai</u>r" and "m<u>a</u>re", or halfway between "bed" and "bade".
î - as in "s<u>ea</u>" and "l<u>ee</u>".
i - as in "caut<u>io</u>n" and "mot<u>io</u>n".
o - as in "c<u>o</u>ne" and "l<u>oa</u>d" but with no off glide: [o] not [o^u].
u - as in "s<u>oo</u>t" and "f<u>oo</u>t".
û - as in "b<u>oo</u>t" and "wh<u>o</u>".

The consonants are as follows:

b - as in "<u>b</u>oy".
c - as in "<u>J</u>ohn" and "<u>j</u>oke".
ç - as in "<u>ch</u>unk" and "pea<u>ch</u>" *.
d - as in "<u>d</u>og".
f - as in "<u>f</u>ire".
g - as in "<u>g</u>irl".
h - as in "<u>h</u>ouse", but also a similar sound made far back in the throat.
j - as in "mea<u>s</u>ure" and "sei<u>z</u>ure".
k - as in "<u>c</u>ar" and "<u>k</u>ilo" *.
1 - as in "<u>l</u>ad".
m - as in "<u>m</u>an".
n - as in "ma<u>n</u>".
p - as in "<u>p</u>eg" *.
q - like [k] but far back on the soft palate.
r - as in "th<u>r</u>ill" with a Scottish accent. Both trilled [r] and flapped

[r] occur in most dialects. In initial position [r] is always trilled. In other positions trilled [r] will be written as [rr] in these lessons. Most Kurdish writers do not use this convention to distinguish the two.

s - as in "sad".

ş - as in "shut" and "hush".

t - as in "toy" *.

v - as in "voice".

w - as in "water".

x - as in the Scottish "loch" and the German "ach".

y - as in "yes".

z - as in "zoo".

* There are significant variants of these sounds that are separate phonemes (aspirated, unaspirated and pharyngealized) but the latin alphabet doesn't distinguish among them.

1.2 - Stress

Nouns and adjectives are stressed on their last syllables. The first syllables of proper nouns in the vocative are stressed. Stress does not fall on suffixes except for "-an" (plural oblique suffix) and "-tir" (comparative ending). The negation prefix "ne-" is stressed (whether on adjectives or on verbs.) The prefix "bi-" (imperative & subjunctive prefix) is stressed. Verbs generally take their stress on the last syllable except if they have personal endings, which are never stressed.

Proper stress can only be learned by mixing with Kurds and then listening to and repeating the way they speak.

1.3 - Simple Sentences

To form basic simple sentences one needs to have a subject, know the verb "to be" and know some basic vocabulary. The subject usually comes at the beginning and the verb at the end of the sentence. Note that the verb "to be" changes if the subject preceding it ends in a vowel. Questions are formed by stress and voice inflection.

1.4 - Personal Pronouns (Direct Case)

ez - I

tu - you (sing.)

ew- he/she/it (that)

(ev - this, these)

em - we

hun - you (pl.)

ew - they (those)

1.5 - Verb: "to be" (present tense)

ez im - I am
tu î - you are
ew e -he/she/it is

em in - we are
hun in - you (pl.) are
ew in - they are

"To be" Following vowels:

ez ... me - I am
tu ... yî - you are
ew ... ye - he/she/it is

em ... ne - we are
hun ... ne - you are
ew ... ne - they/those are

1.6 - Examples of Simple Sentences in Present Tense

Ew şîr e. - That is milk.
Ew şîr e? - Is that milk? (note that only intonation distinguishes this sentence from the first.)
Ev zilam in. - These are men..
Ew mamoste ye. - That is a teacher, or, she/he is a teacher.
Ev kî ye? - Who is this?
Ew kî ye? - Who is that?
Ev çay u şekir e. - This is tea and sugar.
Ew nan u nîvisk e. - That is bread and butter.
Ew pîrek in. - Those/they are women.
Ev pîrek e. - This is (the) woman.
Ev nan e. - This is bread.
Ew goşt e. - That is meat.
Ew xwendekar in. - Those are students.
Hun xwendekar in? - Are you students?
Ew çi ye? - What is that? What is he?
Ev masî ye - This is fish.
Tu kî yî? - Who are you?
Ew kî ne? - Who are they?
Em mamoste ne. - We are teachers.
Ez Tarik im. - I am Tarik.
Tu karker î? - Are you a labourer/worker?
"Ez rê, rastî û hayat im" (Yuh. 14:6). - "I am (the) way, (the) truth and (the) life" (John 14:6).
"Ez qiyamet im û hayat im" (Yuh. 11:25). - "I am (the) resurrection and (the) life" (John 11:25).

1.7 - Case

The case of a word shows its grammatical relationship to the rest of the sentence (ie., whether it is acting or being acted upon, etc.). Case in Kurmanji is not difficult, in that it only has three: the vocative, the direct and the oblique case. We will examine the vocative case in Chapter 9. This leaves the direct and oblique cases.

1.8 - Direct Case

In the beginning the direct case may be thought of as similar to the nominative case in English. Words in the direct case can be the subject of the verb. It is the person or thing doing the acting as opposed to the one being acted upon. Like English, the direct case does not take any special ending; ie., it is the unmarked case.

The personal pronouns in 1.4. are all in the direct case. There are good reasons for not calling this case "nominative" which will be treated in 4.3.

1.9 - Oblique Case

The oblique case takes care of most other case functions such as direct object, indirect object, object of a preposition, etc. The oblique case is a marked case, meaning that it is often evidenced by some ending or internal alteration of a word or both.

1.10 - Oblique Case Personal Pronouns

min - me, mine   me - us, ours
te - you (singular), yours   we - you (plural), yours
wî - him/it, his/its   wan- them, theirs
wê - her/it, hers/its

1.11 - Uses of the Oblique case

A word is put in the oblique case:

1) when it is the object of a preposition:

ji min - from me   liba me - next to us
ji te - from you   liba we - next to you (pl.)
ji wî - from him   linav wan - among them

2) when it is the object of the verb (at least in nonpast tenses):

> Ez te dikujim - I kill (am killing) you. (I you kill)
> ez wî vedixwim - I drink (am drinking) it. (I it drink)

3) when it is subjected to another word in a genitive relationship called "izafe". The word in focus is linked by a connecting vowel to the following word, to which it is subject (by which it is further defined and restricted). That following word, if it is a noun or pronoun will always be in the oblique case (see chapter 2).

> dest-ê min - my hand (lit. hand of me)
> xuh-a wî - his sister (lit. sister of him)

1.12 - Masculine and Feminine Nouns

Like French and Arabic, Kurdish nouns are divided into masculine and feminine. Unlike Arabic, there is no rule of thumb by which one can identify a particular noun as being either masculine or feminine. One has to learn this about every noun individually.

Feminine nouns take a different oblique case ending than masculine nouns do. (Later you will see that gender is differentiated in other ways as well.)

1.13 - Singular Feminine Nouns and the Oblique Case

Singular feminine nouns in the oblique case receive the suffix "-ê"

> av (f.) - water
> ji avê - from the water ("av" is object of prep. "ji")
> li avê - in the water ("av" is object of prep, "li")
> ez avê vedixwim - I am drinking water ("av" is object of verb "drinking")

1.14 - Singular Masculine Nouns and the Oblique Case

Masculine singular nouns in the oblique case receive the suffix "-î" but only under certain conditions, such as when the indefinite article suffix "ek" also accurs: ji mirov-ek-î (from a [certain] man), or with a deictic: ji vi mirov-î (from this man). Otherwise the oblique case suffix does not occur.

ji mirov - from the man (mirov is object of prep, ji)
li goşt - in the meat

Note that many speakers of Kurmanji "internalize" to varying degrees depending on the dialect, the masculine oblique ending when applying it to words with the vowel "a" or "e" so that such vowels become "ê". This change is not restricted to nouns modified by deictics or the indefinite article.

ji nên - from the bread (nan + î = nên)
li xênî - in the house (xanî + î = xênî)
ji bajêr - from the city (bajar + î = bajêr)
li dêst - in the hand (dest + î = dêst)

1.15 - Plural Nouns (both masc. and fem.) in the Oblique Case

Oblique masculine and feminine nouns are treated the same way when plural: the suffix "-an" is added to both.

ji kitêban - from the books (kitêb = feminine)
ji keran - from the donkeys (ker = masculine)

1.16 - The Demonstrative Pronouns in Oblique Case

The demonstrative pronouns are divided into two basic categories as shown by the direct case forms "ev" (this/these) for things nearby and "ew" (that/those) for things farther away. In the direct case the demonstrative pronouns for both feminine and masculine nouns, whether they indicate a single thing or a number of things remain "ev", and "ew".

In the oblique case distinctions are made between the masculine, feminine and plural. The masculine oblique case for "ev" (this) is "vî", and the feminine form is "vê". "Ew" (that) becomes "wî" and "wê" in the masculine and feminine respectively. The plural forms "ev" (these) and "ew" (those) are "van" and "wan" respectively in the oblique case. Notice the overlap between these demonstrative pronouns and the personal pronouns of sections 1.4 and 1.10.

Ch. 10 deals with these demonstratives, or deictic words in more detail.

ji vî mirovî - from this man (masc.)
ji vê kitêbê - from this book (fem.)

ji van kitêban - from these books (pl.)
ji van mirovan - from those men (pl.)

Notice the coordination (agreement) between the demonstrative pronouns and the case endings on the nouns:

vî... - î
vê... - ê
van... - an

Proverb - Gotina Xweş

Nan u mast, xwarina birast.

Bread and yoghurt is a good/correct meal.

Chapter 2

Izafe and the Indefinite Article

2.1 - Izafe

Izafe is a grammatical feature found in Persian, Arabic, and Ottoman Turkish, as well as in Kurdish. The word means "addition" in Arabic. With reference to Iranian languages, like Kurmanji, izafe is a suffix (or set of suffixes) which binds the word to the following word in either a genitive or a descriptive relationship. It is the "glue" that bonds words into noun phrases.

The basic order of elements in the construction is: headnoun, izafe suffix, modifier. The modifier can be another noun, a pronoun, an adjective or an entire noun phrase.

> modifier = noun: çav-ê ker (eye-of donkey, or donkey's eye)
> modifier = pronoun: çav-ê min (eye-of me, or my eye)
> modifier = adjective: çav-ê şîn (eye-of blue, or blue eye)
> modifier = noun phrase: çav-ê kurr-ê min (eye-of son of me, or my son's eye)

Note: For clarity we here show the izafe suffix separated by a hyphen, though it is normally written as part of the word with no hyphen.

2.2 - Masculine Izafe

Add the suffix "-ê" to the noun followed by the modifier. Note that this *masculine* izafe "ê" looks just like the *feminine* oblique case ending "ê"! Note also that for possession, one employs this construction: possessed noun, izafe suffix and oblique case pronoun.

> çav-ê min - my eye
> mamostay-ê te - your teacher ("y" is a buffer between word ending in a vowel and izafe suffix)

19

bav-ê wî - his father
ker-ê me - our donkey
kurr-ê we - your boy, your (pl.) son

2.3 - Femine Izafe

Add the suffix "-a" to the noun followed by the modifier.

qelem-a min - my pen
bêvil-a te - your nose
kitêb-a wê - her book
kecik-a wan - their daughter
reng-a avê - the colour of the water

Note that when the modifier is a noun, it must be in the oblique case (c.p. 2.2 & 1.13)

2.4 - Plural Izafe

In the plural no distinction is made between masculine and feminine. All plural nouns receive the suffix "-ên", followed by the modifier.*

kitêb-ên min - my books (kiteb f.)
bav-ên me - our fathers (bav m.)
keçik-ên we - your daughters (pl. f.)
kurr-ên te - your sons (pl. m.)

* There is considerable variation in the form of the plural izafe suffix from one dialect of Kurmaji to another. Some say "-êt", some "-êd" and many say "-ê" which makes it homophonous with masculine (singular) izafe.

2.5 - Izafe with adjectives

Adjectives always follow what they describe, the noun receiving the appropriate izafe suffix.

çav-ê reş - the black eye
Kitêb-a Reş - the Black Book (Holy Book of the Yezidis)
Kitêb-a Muqaddes - the Holy Book (the Bible)
keçik-a mezin - the big (old) daughter
kurr-ê biçûk - the small son
bêvil-a drêj - the long nose

çav-ên sor - the red eyes (indicates great anger)
nan-ê germ - the warm bread
nan-ê teze - the fresh bread
masîyê mezin - the big fish ("-y-" is buffer for nouns ending in vowels)

2.6 - Izafe with Head Noun and Noun Modifier

In the case of a noun modifying another noun, the head noun receives the izafe suffix and the modifier is in the oblique case, i.e., nan-ê keçikê (the girl's bread). Note that the "-ê" on "nan" is the izafe ending for a masculine word. The "-ê" on "keçik", however, is the oblique case ending for a feminine word. This must be noted carefully, as it can lead to misunderstandings. *The same ending "-ê" is used both as a masculine izafe suffix and as a feminine oblique case ending.* In order to distinguish which ending is before you, it helps to know whether a given noun is masculine or feminine. It can also help to ask yourself whether the following word can be modifying the previous one to form a noun phrase.

hevalê keçikê - the girl's boyfriend
hevala keçikê - the girl's girlfriend
bavê hevala xuha min - my sister's girlfriend's father.*
qelema kurr - the boy's pen

* Note the embedding of whole noun phrases: bav-ê (heval-a (xuh-a min)) - father-of (friend-of (sister-of me))

2.7 - Noun Phrases with both the Possessor and an Adjective

In a phrase which combines both a possessor and an adjective the possessor comes first after the head noun (connected of course by the appropriate izafe suffix). Then the possessor also receives the appropriate SECONDARY izafe suffix and is followed by the adjective. The secondary izafe suffixes are: masc. - "î", fem. - "e", plural - "î".

masculine: dest-ê min-î rast - my right hand
feminine: qelem-a min-e drêj - my long pen
kitêb-en min-î nû - my new book.
kitêb-n-e min-î nû - some new books of mine.

Alternatively, the ordinary izafe suffixes may be written as the separate words "yê", "ya", and "yên" following the possessor. This form is more emphatic:

masculine: dest-ê min yê rast - my hand, the *right* one.
feminine: qelem-a min ya drêj - my pen, the *long* one.
plural: kitêb-ên min yên nu - my books, the *new* ones.

The exclamation "That's mine!" is "Ya min e!".

2.8 - Indefinite Article

The indefinite article (comparable to English "a, an") is formed in Kurdish by adding the suffix "-ek" on the end of the noun it modifies. There is no such thing as a definite article (the)--all nouns which do not have the indefinite article are definite. The plural indefinite suffix (some) is "-ne".

kurr - son, the son » kurr-ek - a son
hêk - egg, the egg » hêk-ek - an egg
tilih - finger, the finger » tilih-ek - a finger
kitêb-ne - some books
xanî-ne - some houses

2.9 - Izafe and the Indefinite Article

When a noun is modified by both the indefinite article and another modifier, the indefinite article is attached directly to the noun and then the appropriate *secondary* izafe suffix is attached as the connector to the modifier which follows. Exceptional is the plural secondary izafe in the immediate context of the plural indefinite article; in that case the plural secondary izafe is "-e".

kurrê min - my son (normal izafe) » kurr-ek-î min - a son of mine
(sec. izafe)
çavê min - my eye (normal izafe) » çav-ek-î min - one of my eyes
(sec. izafe)
hêka min - my egg (normal izafe) » hêk-ek-e min - one of my eggs
(sec. izafe)

2.10 - Secondary Izafe

In sections 2.7 and 2.9 we have seen uses of secondary izafe. You may be asking yourself what the general rule for its use might be. Basically, when you want to add a modifier to something that is already modified, you need to use secondary izafe. For example, "xaniyek" (a house) already includes the indefinite article, which in a sense modifies "house".

Therefore, any additional modifier would require secondary izafe: "xaniyek-î biçûk" (a small house), "xaniyek-î min" (a house of mine).

If we want to add an adjective to a noun that is already modified by a noun, pronoun or adjective, secondary izafe is required:

> kitêb-a mekteb-e nû - new school book
> kitêb-a min-e nû - my new book
> kitêb-a baş-e nû - good new book
> kitêbne başî nû - some good, new books
> xanîne başî nû - some good, new houses
> "Ev kurrê minî delal e" (Luqa 9:35). - "This is my beloved son " (Luke 9:35).

Proverb - Gotina Xweş

Nan u dew xwarina derew

Bread and buttermilk is a false (unsatisfying) meal.

Chapter 3

Verbs

3.1 - Verb Stems: the Infinitive and the Imperative

Every Kurmanji verb has two separate stems from which all its various forms (with a few rare exceptions) can be derived. Neither of the stems can be consistently predicted from the form of the other. Just as one must memorize the three principle parts of irregular (or strong) verbs in English or German, in Kurmanji one must memorize two principle parts of every verb.

All verb forms can normally be derived either from the infinitive, which contains the past stem, or from the imperative, which contains the present stem. This is why the dictionary lists both forms of the verb -- first the infinitive, then the imperative. The infinitive and imperative forms of the verb can be quite different.

The infinitive always ends in "-n", and the imperative usually begins with "bi-" and ends in "-e".

> çûn, biçe! - to go, go!
> kirin, bike! - to do/make, do it!/make it!

3.2 - Verb Stem for the Present Tenses

The present stem of a verb is derived by dropping the "bi-" prefix, if there is one, and the "-e" suffix off the imperative (second dictionary form) of the verb.

> ketin, bikeve - to fall: bikeve » bi-kev-e » kev. Thus, present tense stem of "ketin, bikeve" is "kev".

> çûn, biçe - to go: biçe » bi-ç-e » ç. Thus, present tense stem of "çûn, biçe" is simply "ç".

24

man, bimîne - to stay, to remain: bimîne » bi-mîn-e » min. Thus "mîn" is present tense stem.

Note that some imperatives end in a vowel other than "-e". In such cases the vowel is part of the stem:

şiştin, bişo - to wash: bişo » bi-şo » şo.

If an imperative begins with "b-" plus any vowel other than "i", it is likely that the vowel is the beginning of the present stem.

axiftin, baxive - to speak » b-axiv-e.

Note also that not every imperative includes the prefix "bi-", eg., "hildan, hilde", "to raise, lift". In most cases these are old compound verbs where the preverbal element (in this case "hil-") precludes the use of the "bi-" prefix.

3.3 - Simple Present Tense

The simple present indicative of all verbs (both transitive and intransitive) is formed by adding the prefix "di-" to the present stem and the appropriate personal ending similar to those for "to be" (see 1.5). Note that having a present stem that ends in a vowel affects the personal endings differently than does a similar set of conditions with the verb "to be" (1.5).

kirin, bike - to do
ez di-k-im - I do, am doing	em di-k-in - we do, are doing
tu di-k-î - you do, are doing	hun di-k-in -you (pl.) do, are doing
ew di-k-e - he/she does, is doing	ew di-k-in - they do, are doing

Note that when the present stem ends in a vowel, the 3rd singular personal ending is lost.

şiştin, bişo - to wash
ez di-şo-m - I wash, am washing	em di-şo-n - we wash, are washing
tu di-şo-yî - you wash, are washing	hun di-şo-n - you (pl.) wash, are washing
ew di-şo - he washes, is washing	ew di-şo-n -they wash, are washing

jîn, bijî - to live

ez di-jî-m - I live, am alive

tu di-jî - you live, are alive

ew di-jî - he lives, is alive

em di-jî-n - we live, are alive

hun di-jî-n - you (pl.) live, are alive

ew di-jî-n -they live, are alive

Note: Present verb stem is "jî". Second person "î" suffix assimilated into the "î" verb ending in the second person singular and the third person "-e" does not appear either. That is why second and third persons singular look the same.

In at least one verb, the present tense is based on an alternate imperative: çûn, herre (biçe).

çûn, herre - to go

ez di-ç-im - I am going

tu di-ç-î - you are going

ew di-ç-e - he is going

em di-ç-in - we are going

hun di-ç-in - you (pl.) are going

ew di-ç-in - they are going

Various dialects of Kurmanji differ as to which forms are based on the present stem "-ç-" and which forms are based on the stem of the more usual imperative "herre".

If the present stem begins with a vowel, the prefix will change from "di-" to simply "d-", a reflection of the weakness of the vowel "i".

axiftin, baxive - to speak

ez d-axiv-im - I speak, am speaking

tu d-axiv-î - you speak, are speaking

ew d-axiv-e - he speaks, is speaking

em d-axiv-in - we speak, are speaking

hun d-axiv-in - you speak, are speaking

ew d-axiv-in -they speak, are speaking

"Hatin, werre" is an exception to the above rules. Its present tense is formed as follows:

hatin, werre - to come

ez têm - I come, am coming

tu teyî - you come, are coming

ew tê - he comes, is coming

em tên - we come, are coming

hun tên - you (pl.) come, are coming

ew tên - they come, are coming

"anîn, bîne" is similarly exceptional:

anîn, bîne - to bring

ez tînim - I bring, am bringing
tu tînî - you bring, are bringing
ew tîne - he brings, is bringing

em tînin - we bring, are bringing
hun tînin - you bring, are bringing
ew tînin - they bring, are bringing

3.4 - Negation of Present Tense

To negate the present tense simply drop the "di-" prefix and substitute with "na-".

> ez dikevim - I am falling » ez nakevim - I am not falling
> ez dişom - I am washing » ez naşom - I am not washing.

The only two exceptions to this rule are the verbs "zanin, bizane" (to know) and "karin, bikare" (to do). They take "ni-" instead of "na-".

> ez nizanim - I don't know
> ez nikarim - I cannot.

3.5 - Verb of Existence

Though the English verb "to exist" is used relatively seldom, the Kurmanji equivalent, based on the verb "hebûn, hebe" (to be) is quite commonly used for such expressions as "there is (one)", "there are (some)".

> ew heye - he/she/it is, exists
> ew hene - they are, exist
> av heye? - Is there water?
> hêk hene? - Are there eggs?

This verb is also employed with a noun phrase to express possession; no Kurdish equivalent of the verb "to have" exists.

> Sê birayên min hene. -1 have three brothers. (Three brothers-of me exist)
> Kurrikê wî heye. - He has a small son. (Little boy-of him exists)
> Qelema te heye? - Do you have a pencil? (Pencil-of you exists?)

3.6 - The Verb "bûn, bibe" - to be, to become

The verb "bûn, bibe" can express both a state (being) and a process (becoming). When "bûn" is used to describe a state of being it comes after the word which describes its state. If "bun" is used as a process (becoming something) then it comes before that which the subject is becoming.

> Ez maldar bûm. - I was rich.
> Ez bûm maldar. - I became rich.
> Mû, mû, mû, dibe rih. - hair (by) hair (by) hair becomes a beard.

Even the form of this verb differs in the subjunctive depending on whether the meaning is "become" or "be" (see 6.6).

> Xwedê bi we re be. - God be with you.
> Ew bibe qiral. - May he become king.

3.7 - Compound Verbs with Preverbals

Kurdish has a series of compound verbs, i.e., verbs which have a preverbal element attached to their stems. With a few exceptions, these stems are from common verbs. The different preverbals give these verb stems quite different meanings.

Some of the regular preverbals are "ve-", "ra-", "der-", "da-", and "hil-". The present indicative prefix "di-" is normally infixed between the preverbal and the verb stem. In some dialects one may find that the prefix has migrated to the front of the compound, i.e., instead of the normal "ve-di-xwe" (he drinks), one may find "di-vexwe". If the imperative form in the dictionary does not have the "bi-" prefix, one can usually assume that the word is a compound verb.

> vebûn, vebe - to be opened
> vexwarin, vexwe - to drink
> vekirin, veke - to open
>
> rabûn, rabe - to stand up
> rawestan, raweste - to stand (up), to stop
> rakirin, rake - to lift up, to establish,
>
> deranîn, derîne - to take out
> derketin, derkeve - to leave, to set out
> derxistin, derxe - to throw out
> dagirtin, dagre - to fill

28

daketin, dakeve - to come down, descend

Attempts have been made to extract specific meanings for the preverbals. It could be argued that "ra-" means "up", and "der-" "out". However, one encounters so many exceptions that it is impossible to formulate consistent rules of this kind.

3.8 - Preverbals that are Contractions

When used together, certain pronouns and prepositions can be contracted together. These contractions can, in turn, be used as compound verb prefixes.

> li + wî/wê can be contracted to "lê" - in him/her/it
> ji + wî/wê can be contracted to "jê" - from him/her/it
> di + wî/wê can be contracted to "tê" - in him/her/it
> bi + wî/wê can be contracted to "pê" - with him/her/it

These contractions can in turn be used as compound verb prefixes:

> lêxistin, bileyize - to hit, to throw it
> têgihan, bighe - to arrive at/in it, to understand it
> pêxistin, pêxe - to light, to turn it on
> dest pêkirin - to put one's hand to it, to begin it

3.9 - Other Compound Verbs

A great many Kurmanji verbs are compounds comprised of a basic verb preceded by a recognizable word such as an adjective or a noun. The verbs "kirin, bike" (to do) and "bûn, bibe" (to be) are most often used in this way. Sometimes "dan, bide" (to give) is also used to form such a compound.

> kar (work) - karkirin (to work)
> kêm (few) - kêmkirin (to become less, to reduce, to deplete)
> zêde (extra) - zêdebûn (to increase)
> av (water) - avdan (to water/irrigate)

Similarly there are some verbs that must have a similar origin though the first element is not currently used as an independent word.

> hînbûn (learn) - hînkirin (to teach)

29

çêbûn (to come into being) - çêkirin (to create/prepare)

3.10 - List of Some Basic Verbs

çûn, biçe - to go
şiştin, bişo - to wash
kirin, bike - to do, to make
kenîn, bikene - to laugh
jîn, bijî - to live (unfamiliar to speakers of some dialects)
girîn, bigrî - to cry, to weep
ketin, bikeve - to fall
man, bimîne - to stay, to remain
gotin, bibêje - to say
anîn, bîne - to bring
firrîn, bifirre - to fly
hebûn, hebe - to be
zanîn, bizane - to know
bawer kirin - to believe
alîkarî kirin - to help
nimêj kirin - to pray
hazir kirin - to prepare
ava kirin - to thrive, to increase
tijî kirin - to fill
çebûn - to succeed, to be born
gerek bûn - to be in need
hîn bûn - to learn
av dan - to water (plants)
guh dan - to give ear to, to listen
çekirin - to make, fix, repair, prepare (a meal)
derbas bûn - to pass (in the subjunctive form "derbas be" is said to someone not feeling well; it can also mean "to cross" or "to enter")
hatin, werre - to come

Proverb - Gotina xweş
Nan û şîr, xwarina mîr
Bread and milk is a princely meal.

Putting together the three proverbs learned so far makes a little poem:

Nan û mast, xwarina birast,
nan û dew, xwarina derew,
nan û şîr, xwarina mir.

Chapter 4

Past Tense of Verbs

4 .1 - Verb Stem for the Past Tenses

The past stem of a verb is derived by simply dropping the "-in" off the infinitive form (1st dictionary form) of the verb. If the verb stem ends in a vowel then the infinitive will not display the ending "-in"; it will simply display an "-n". This is due to the fact that the vowel "i" is the weakest of Kurdish vowels and disappears whenever it comes in contact with another. In such cases the removal of the "-n" from the infinitive results in the past stem. The verb stem is the same as the third person singular form of the verb in the preterite (simple past) tense. In other words, the third person singular form of this tense has no personal ending (null morpheme).

> şiştin » şişt = he washed
> kirin » kir = he did/he made
> çûn » cu = he went

4.2 - Simple Past Tense of Intransitive Verbs

Simple past tense of intransitive verbs (i.e.,verbs which do not require a direct object) are formed by simply taking the past tense verb stem and adding the "to be" suffixes (see 1.5). The only exception is the 3rd person singular, "he, she, is" which, as noted above, is the same as the simple past stem with no suffix added.

Transitive past tense verbs are also formed this way, but there is an added feature governing their behavior which we will look at later (see 4.3).

> ketin. bikeve - to fall (stem = ket)
>
> | | |
> |---|---|
> | ez ketim - I fell | em ketin - we fell |
> | tu ketî - you (sing.) fell | hun ketin - you (pl.) fell |
> | ew ket - he/she/it fell | ew ketin - they fell |

çûn, biçe - to go (stem = çu)

ez çûm - I went	em çûn - we went
tu çûyî - you (sing.) went	hun çûn - you (pl.) went
ew çû - he/she/it went	ew çûn - they went

Note: If verb stem ends in vowel, then a "y" is added by some writers as a buffer between stem and suffix vowels — see second person singular, "çûyî". It is normally pronounced, however, as one syllable, i.e. as if it were spelled "çûy".

firrîn. bifirre - to fly (past stem = firrî)

ez firrîm - I flew	em firrîn - we flew
tu firrî - you (sing.) flew	hun firrîn - you (pl.) flew
(extra "i" assimilated)	
ew firrî - he/she/it flew	ew firrîn - they flew
("i" part of stem)	

4.3 - Past Tense of Transitive Verbs and Ergativity

Like the past tense of intransitive verbs, the past tense of transitive verbs is based on the past stem, which is found in the infinitve form of the verb (ie., the first dictionary form). However, there is an "ergative" rule which governs transitive verbs in the past tenses which states that:

The subject of a transitive verb in the past tenses is always in the oblique case. The object of the transitive verb in the past tense is in the direct (nominative) case. The verb will agree with the OBJECT in number and person.

Thus the cases and the verb agreement are the opposite of what one gets in the nonpast forms. In nominative-accusative languages the object of the verb would be in the oblique (or accusative) case and the subject in the direct (nominative) case, but in Kurmanji this is reversed — but only in the past tense of transitive verbs.

This "split ergativity" is evidenced in various ways in several other Indo-Iranian languages.

4.4 - Examples of the Transitive Past Tense Verbs

Note that in the examples below the subjects of the verb are all in the oblique case and the objects in the direct case. The verb is conjugated just like the simple past tense of intransitive verbs (see 3.3) except that, since the object of the sentence is in the direct case, they are in agreement with the object, not the subject.

> wî ez ditim - he saw me. "wî" = subject of sentence, but in oblique case because the verb is past tense transitive. "Ez", the object of the verb is in the direct (nominative) case for the same reason. "Dîtim", the verb, agrees in number and person with "ez", its object.

> wî tu dîtî - he saw you
> wî ew dît - he saw it/her/him
> wî em dîtin - he saw us
> wî hun dîtin - he saw you (pl.)
> wî ew dîtin - he saw them
> kê tu dîtî? - Who saw you? (remember, "kî" (who, whom) in the direct case and "kê" (who, whom) in the oblique case, ie. tu kî dît? - whom did you see?)
> kurr keç dît - the boy saw the girl
> keçekê kurr dîtin - a girl saw the boys
> kurrekî keçek dît - a boy saw a girl
> keçan kurr dîtin - the girls saw the boys
> kurran keç dîtin - the boys saw the girls
> kê kurr dîtin - who saw the boys?
> kê doh kurr dîtin? - Who saw the boys yesterday?
> min xwe şişt - I washed myself
> wî xwe şişt - he washed himself
> wan xwe şiştin - they washed themselves ("xwe" had a plural antecedent).

4.5 - Progressive Past Tense

The progressive past tense (I was going etc.) is formed by simply adding the indicative prefix "di-" before the simple past tense.

> ez di-ket-im - I was falling
> tu di-ket-î - you were falling
> ew di-çû - he was going
> em di-firrî-n - we were flying, etc.

4.6 - Negation of Past Tense

To negate the past tense add the prefix "ne-". i.e. just prefix "ne-" to the simple past tense of the verb. Note that the vowel of this negative prefix differs from that in 3.4.

> ez ne-çû-m - I didn't go
> tu ne-çûyi - you didn't go, etc.
> wî ez nedîtim - he didn't see me.

4.7 - Negation of Past Progressive Tense

Unlike the present tense, where the negative prefix replaces the indicative prefix "di-", the two co-occur in negating the past progressive:

> ez ne-di-çûm - I wasn't going.
> em ne-di-firrîn - we weren't flying.

Gotina xweş- Proverb

Mala Xwedê ava.

May God's possessions increase/prosper

(A blessing or exclamation said upon the birth of a child
or other occasion when one wants to express praise to God.)

34

Chapter 5

The Perfect Tenses

5.1 - The Present Perfect Tense

By the perfect tenses we mean verbs that refer to action completed in the past. The present perfect tense denotes an action which happened in the past, the results of which are still felt at the present.

In Kurmanji the perfect tenses are formed with a special participle. This special participle is made by taking the infinitive and dropping the final "n" but keeping the preceding vowel, even if it is the weak vowel "i". For the present perfect tense one then adds the personal endings to this special participle. Since this special participle always ends in a vowel, the 2nd form of the personal endings, i.e. those used after vowels, is used (see 1.5). The 2nd person singular "-yî" ending, however, becomes a "-ye", making it homophonous with the 3rd person singular.

The formation of regular participles is covered in 8.1.

      <u>ketin, bikeve - to fall</u>
      ez ketime - I have fallen   em ketine - we have fallen
      tu ketiye - you have fallen   hun ketine - you (pl.) have fallen
      ew ketiye - he/she/it has fallen   ew ketine - they have fallen

      <u>çûn - to go</u>
      ez çûme - I have gone   em çûne - we have gone
      tu çûye - you have gone   hun çûne - you (pl.) have gone
      ew çûye - he/she/it has gone   ew çûne - they have gone

5.2 - Present Perfect Tense and Transitive Verbs

For transitive verbs in the present perfect use the oblique case for the subject of the verb. Perfect tenses are also subject to ergativity (see 4.3).

Min ew dîtiye - I have seen him/her/it.
Wê ew dîtiye - she has seen him/her/it.
Wan ew dîtiye - they have seen him/her/it.
Wî ez dîtime - He has seen me.
Wî ew dîtine - He has seen them.
Te sêv firoştiye? - Have you sold the apple?
Me sêv kirrîne - We have bought the apples.

5.3 - Pluperfect (or Past Perfect) Tense

The pluperfect tense is the "past in the past". In Kurmanji the pluperfect is used much like it is used in English, i.e. to designate an event or a state which took place before a specific time in the past (i.e. When he called, I had gone.)

The pluperfect is formed with the special participle and the verb "bûn, bibe" (to be, to become). To that participle one adds the simple past form of "bûn" conjugated to agree with the appropriate referent, i.e. the subject if the verb is intransitive, the object if transitive.

hatin » hati + bûn = (they, we, you (pl.)) had come
xwarin » xwari + bûn = (they, we, you (pl.)) had eaten
dan » da + bûn = (they, we, you (pl.)) had given
çûn » çû + bûm = I had gone
kenîn » kenî + bûyî = you (sing.) had laughed
ketin » keti + bû = he/she/it had fallen, etc.

Intransitive verbs (verb agrees with subject);

Ew hati bû. - He had come.
Ez keti bûm. - I had fallen.
Tu keti bûyî. - You had fallen, etc.

Transitive verbs (verb agrees with object):

min (ew) dîti bû. - I had seen it.
te (ew) dîti bû. - You had seen it
wî (ew) dîti bû. - He had seen it. etc.

Remember, the reason "bû" does not change in these three examples is because the object "ew" remaines the same. When the object of the transitive verb in the past tense changes, "bûn" will change accordingly.

Wî ez dîti bûm. - He had seen me.
Min hun dîti bûn. - I had seen you.
Wan ez dîti bûm. - They had seen me.
Min tu dîti bûyî. - I had seen you.
Min kitêb xwendi bûn, hingî ez çûm. - I had read the books, then I went.
Min (ew) nizani bû... - I had not known (that)...

Gotina Xweş - Proverb

Mû bi mû rihek çêdibe.

Hair by hair a beard grows/comes into being.

Chapter 6

The Subjunctive and the Conditional

6.1 - The Subjunctive Mood

The subjunctive mood means that a verb represents an action or state of being not as a fact but as contingent, doubtful or possible. To create the subjunctive form in Kurdish one simply drops the suffix "e" from the imperative and adds the personal endings.

The prefix "bi-" is common to the imperative and subjunctive forms and is referred to as the subjunctive prefix. The best way to distinguish the two is, of course, by context. Also, the imperative, being always in the second person, is restricted in the number of different personal endings it displays.

The only way to distinguish the third person singular subjunctive from the imperative is from the context. In compound verbs the "bi-" prefix is not used (like their imperative forms).

> dîtin, bibîne - to see
> subj. form: bibînim - (would) that I (could) see.
>   bibînî - (would) that you (could) see.
>   bibîne - (would) that he (could) see.
>   etc.

> vexwarin, vexwe - to drink
> subj. form: vexwim - (would) that I (could) drink.
>   vexwî - would that you (could) drink.
>   etc.

6.2 - Subjunctive Used with Helping Verbs

Helping verbs express the ability to do something, knowledge of something, wishing or wanting to do something, and being advised about or warned against something. In Kurdish, helping verbs are followed by the subjunctive form of the verb.

Note that helping verbs are divided into two categories: those which are conjugated (xwestin - to want, karîn - to be able, zanîn - to know), and those which are not (gerek - should, divê - ought, lazim e - must, and mecbûr - definitely must, incumbent that).

6.3 - Examples of the Subjunctive & Conjugated Helping Verbs

Ez karim bibînim. - I can see.
Ez zanim bajom. - I know how to drive.
Ez dixwazim hînbibim. - I want to learn.
Tu karî bikenî? - Can you laugh?
Erê ez karim bikenim. - Yes I can laugh.
Tu dixwazî Kurmanjî bêjî? - You want to speak Kurdish?
Erê, ez dixwazim Kurmanjî bêjim. - Yes, I want to speak Kurdish.
Tu zanî bixwînî? - Do you know how to read?
Erê, ez zanim bixwînim. - Yes, I know how to read.
Tu karî wî hildî? - Are you able to lift it? (hildan, hilde is a compound verb and therefore the subjunctive prefix "bi-" is missing.)

6.4 - Examples of the Subjunctive & Unconjugated Helping Verbs

Gerek tu bixwî. - You should eat.
Gerek tu nexwî. - You should not eat.
Divê tu bajoyî. - You ought to drive.
Lazim e tu bibînî. - You must see! (It is necessary that you see.)
Mecbûr tu bixwî. - You must eat!
Lazim e tu Kurmanji baxivî? - Is it necessary that you speak Kurdish?

Note: Of these three only "divê" is Kurdish; "gerek" is Turkish and "lazim" and "mecbûr" are Arabic. In fact all three are used in Kurmanji.

6.5 - Negation of the Subjunctive Mood

To negate the subjunctive replace the prefix "bi-" with "ne-". *Remember, "na-" negates normal present tense indicative verbs and "ne-" subjunctive verbs.* "ni-" is used for verbs like "kari" (to be able to) and "zani" which have an "a" following the first consonant.

Lazim e tu nebînî. - It is necessary that you not see.

It is also possible to negate the "helping verb".

Ne mecbûr e tu bixwî. - It is not necessary that you eat.

6.6 - Exceptions and Dialectal Differences

The verbs "hatin, werre" (to come) and "çûn, herre" (to go) are exceptions to the above stated rules.

"Hatin, werre" has two forms of the subjunctive: the regular and the alternative form. The first form (werre) is often used to indicate the imperative mood, and the alternative form for the subjunctive mood. Some dialects use only one or the other of these two forms exclusively.

hatin. werre - to come

1st subjunctive:	alternative:
ez werim	ez bêm
tu werî	tu beyî
ew were	ew bê
em werin	em bên
hun werin	hun bên
ew werin	ew bên

The subjunctive forms of "çûn, herre" (to go) that are based on the imperative appear to be remnants of a different verb, much like the use of English "went" as a past tense for "go". In some dialects the alternative subjunctive is used, which is based on the same root as "çûn". In all cases, the imperative seems to remain "herre".

subjunctive of çûn. herre - to go   *alternative:*

ez herrim	em herrin	biçim	biçin
tu herrî	hun herrin	biçî	biçin
ew herre	ew herrin	biçe	biçe

Note the the two subjunctive forms of "bûn, bibe". These two forms are not dialectal differences but actually denote the difference between "to be" and "to become".

subjunctive of "bûn, be" when meaning "to be"

ez bim	em bin
tu bî (or be)	hun bin
ew be	ew bin

<u>subjunctive of "bûn, bibe" when meaning "to become"</u>

ez bibim	em bibin
tu bibî	hun bibin
ew bibe	ew bibin

Note: Some dialects may only have one of these sets of subjunctive forms to cover both usages.

6.7 - Conditional and Purpose Clauses

Conditional and purpose clauses are introduced by appropriate conjuctions and exhibit subjunctive form. See also 11.3-11.4.

> Ez diçim xwendegehê dajiboy ez bixwînim. - I go to the university in order to study.
> Ez dixwînim dajiboy bibim mamoste - I am studying in order to become a teacher.
> Go ez bibim mamoste... - If I become a teacher...

6.8 - Second Subjunctive and Contrafactual Conditionals

A contrafactual conditional is a type of conditional used when expressing a state of being which is not or was not, nor can be. In English we would express a contrafactual by beginning a sentence with "If I were...", or, "If I had been..."

In Kurdish, contrafactual conditionals are formed through the use of a second, slightly different type of subjunctive, logically enough called the 2nd subjunctive endings.

> *2nd Subjunctive endings:*
> -ama
> -ayî
> -a
> -ana
> -ana
> -ana

"bûn, bibe" - to be in the 2nd subjunctive (if I were... etc.)

2nd Subjuntive	Shortened form	Normal Subjunctive
ez biwama	ez bama	ez bim
tu biwayî	tu bayî	tu bî
ew biwa	ew ba	ew bê
em biwana	em bana	em bin
hun biwana	hun bana	hun bin
ew biwana	ew bana	ew bin

"bûn, bibe" - to be in the pluperfect 2nd subjunctive (if I had been... etc.)

Ez bû bama	em bû bana
tu bû bayi	hun bû bana
ew bû ba	ew bû bana

Gotina Xweş - Proverb

Xebera xweş, xweş e, xebera nexweş kula reş e.

A good word is good, a bad word is a black wound (pain).

Chapter 7

Future Tense and Passive Mood

7.1 - Formation of the Future Tense

To express future tense, one puts the verb in the subjunctive; ie. take the imperative (2nd dictionary) form of the verb, drop the "-e" and add the personal endings. However, to indicate the future and not the subjunctive, add the suffix "-ê" to the pronoun which is the subject of the verb.

> xwarin, bixwe - to eat
> ezê bixwim - I am going to eat
> tê (=tu+yê) bixwî - you are going to eat
> ewê bixwe - he/she/it is going to eat
> emê bixwin - we are going to eat
> hunê bixwin - you (pl.) are going to eat
> ewê bixwin - the are going to eat

If the subject of the future tense verb is a noun and not a pronoun, the future tense indicator "wê" (in some dialects "dê") follows it. It stands alone, ie. is not attached to the noun.

> Azad wê bixwe - Azad will eat.
> Mamoste wê bê. - The professor will come

"wê" usually comes after the noun, but in some dialects one might find it before its subject: "Wê Azad bixwe" - "Azad will eat".

> Ezê te bikujim - I will kill you (note, "te" is in the oblique case as it is the object of the verb).
> Ezê nên bidim te - I will give the bread to you.
> Kurrê te wê bijî - Your son will live.
> "Werre cem min... û ezê rihatiyê bidim we" (Matta 11:28). - Follow me and I will give you rest (Mat. 11:28).

Note: Whether a verb in the future tense is transitive or intransitive makes no difference. The direct case (nominative case) is always used for the subject of the verb. The verb agrees with the subject.

7.2 - Formation of the Passive

A verb is passive when the subject does not act, but is acted upon. *In Kurdish the passive construction is formed by conjugating the verb "hatin" (to come) appropriately for the context and by following that with the infinitive of the verb which is to be passivized.* It is, of course, only possible to make transitive verbs passive.

7.3 - Examples of Passives

> ez hatim girêdan - I was tied (up)
> tu hatî girêdan - you were tied (up)
> ew hat girêdan - he was tied (up)
> em hatin girêdan - we were tied (up)
> hun hatin girêdan - you (pl.) were tied (up)
> ew hatin girêdan - they were tied (up)
> Mirov tê kuştin. - The person is being killed.
> Ez têm kuştin. - I am being killed.
> Tu teyî kuştin. - You were killed.
> Sêv tên xwarin. - The apples are being eaten.
> Ji Birahîm re tê gotin dost ê Xwedê û ji Musa re tê gotin xeberdanê Xwedê. - Abraham is called "friend of God" and Moses is called "companion of God" (more like: who had conversation with God).

7.4 - Future Tense Passive Construction

The passive in the future tense is formed by putting the verb "hatin" in the subjunctive, the main verb in the infinitive, and the future marker ("-ê" or "wê") on the subject. Remember: "hatin" has 2 alternative subjunctive forms (see 6.6).

> Ezê bêm girêdan. - I will be tied
> Tê beyî girêdan. - You will be tied.
> Mirov wê bê girêdan. - The person will be tied.
> Mirov wê were girêdan - The person will be tied.

7.5 - Past Tense Passive Construction

Although the past tenses of transitive verbs are affected by ergativity (ie., the fact that the subjects of past tense transitive verbs are in the oblique case and the objects in the direct case; see ch. 4), this is not the case in the passive construction. The reason for this is that the subject of the passive is also the thing acted upon, and consequently it remains in the direct case. Also, the verb being conjugated, "hatin", is not transitive although the infinitve that follows is. Thus, to form the past tense passive construction, the subject of the sentence is followed by the past tense of "hatin" conjugated according to the subject. "Hatin" is followed by the infinitive of the main verb of the sentence. An "-e" is sometimes added to "hatin" for euphonic reasons.

> Sêv hate xwarin. - The apple was eaten.
> Ez hatime kuştin. - I was killed, (often the "i" in "hatin" is dropped: "Ez hatme kustin.")

Note: Due to the euphonic "-e" added to "hatin" in the past tense passive construction it looks like the perfect passive tense. In some forms they are indistinguishable.

> Sêv hatiye xwarin. - The apple has been eaten.
> Sêv hate xwarin. - The apple was eaten.
> Ez hatim(e) dîtin. - I was seen.
> Ez hatime dîtin. - I have been seen.

7.6 - Passive in the Perfect Tenses

As with any other tense, the perfect and the pluperfect (past perfect) may also be applied to verbs in the passive mood. One simply puts "hatin" (to go) in the appropriate tense (see sec. 5.3) and follows it with the infinitive of the verb to be passivized.

> Sêv hati bû xwarin. - The apple had been eaten.
> Sêv hatiye xwarin. - The apple has been eaten.

Gotina xweş - Proverb

Mirov bi zimanê xwe tê girêdan.

A person is tied up (bound, obligated) by his own tongue.

45

Chapter 8

Participles, Verbal & Abstract Nouns, Adjectives

8.1 - Formation of Participles

Participles make adjectives out of verbs. To make a participle you take the past stem and add "î". Participles based on transitive verbs generally have passive meaning while those based on intransitive verbs have active meaning.

Infinitive	Past stem	Participle
ketin	ket	ketî (fallen)
runiştin	runişt	runiştî (sitting, having sat)
şiştin	şişt	şiştî (washed, as in "the washed clothes)"

If the past stem of a particular verb ends in a long vowel, then place a "y" between the verb stem and the partciple ending as a buffer.

man	ma	mayî (remaining, having remained)
çûn	çû	çûyî (gone)

If the stem ends in an "î", then there is no need to add another "i".

girîn	girî	girî (crying)

When the participle modifies a noun the izafe will be added to the noun as with any modified noun and adjective.

> kurrê ketî - the fallen boy
> keça runiştî - the sitting girl
> cilên şistî - the washed clothes

When the noun modified is missing, the izafe can still be present, referring back to the missing noun. (This is true of any adjective, not just of participles.)

> yê ketî - the fallen (one)
> yê runiştî - the sitting (one)
> yên şiştî - the washed (ones)

8.2 - Infinitives as Nouns

In Kurmanji all infinitive forms of the verb can be used as nouns. These nouns are all feminine; they take the feminine izafe and oblique case ending.

> gotin, bêje - to say » gotin - a saying » gotina xwes, - a proverb (pleasant word)
> Xwendina te baş e. - Your reading is good.
> Emê dest bi xwendinê bibin. - We will begin (the) reading.

8.3 - Abstract Nouns

Abstract nouns are formed by adding the suffix "-î" to adjectives. When the adjective already ends in a vowel, add "-tî". These nouns are likewise always feminine.

> azad - free » azadî - freedom
> hejar - poor » hejarî - poverty
> nexweş - sick » nexweşî - sickness
> birçî - hungry » birçîtî - hunger ("t" is the buffer between adjective ending in a vowel and abstract noun ending.)
> spehî - beautiful » spehîtî - beauty

Sometimes the suffix "-î" appears as "-ayî", "-anî", or "-atî". It may be significant that many of the adjectives which take the longer endings are monosyllabic.

> dûr - far » dûrayî - distance
> dirêj - long » dirêjayî - length
> germ - warm » germayî - warmth
> mêr - man » mêranî - manliness
> xort - youth » xortanî - youthfulness
> pirr - many » pirranî - majority, most

mirov - person » mirovatî - humanity, humanness
kirîv - godparent » kirîvatî - godparenthood

8.4 - Making Adjectives out of Nouns

Adjectives made from nouns are formed by adding "-î" to the noun.

hesin - iron » hesinî - ironlike, made of iron.
zîv - silver » zîvî - silvery, made of silver.
zêr - gold » zêrî - golden.

8.5 - Making Nouns out of Nouns

Sometimes one noun is derived from another by the addition of the suffix "-î", most often indicating where someone comes from.

bajar - city » bajarî - urbanite
gund - village » gundî - villager
Iran - Iran » Iranî - Iranian

Gotinên pêşiya - Sayings of the ancestors
(another word for "proverbs")

Xwîn nabe av.

Blood doesn't become water.

Chapter 9

Numbers, Comparatives and Superlatives

9.1 - The Numbers

yek - one	şanzde - sixteen
didu, du - two	hivde - seventeen
sisê, sê - three	hijde - eighteen
çar - four	nozde - nineteen
pênc - five	bist - twenty
şeş - six	sî, sih (dialectal variants) - thirty
heft - seven	çil - fourty
heşt - eight	pêncî, pêncih (dialectal variants) - fifty
neh - nine	şeşt - sixty
deh - ten	hefta - seventy
yanzde - eleven	heşta - eighty
dwanzde - twelve	not - ninety
sêzde - thirteen	sed - one hundred
çarde - fourteen	hezar - one thousand
panzde - fifteen	

If dido (two) and sisê (three) modify a following noun, the first syllable of these numbers falls off.

du zilam, sê zilam - two men, three men.

9.2 - Numbers and Gender

The numbers are sometimes used as substantives (nouns) and when they are, they must be declined (marked for case) like any other noun. In order to decline a noun one must know whether it is masculine or feminine. In Kurmanji, the following rules hold for numbers used as substantives:

1. The number "one" and all numbers ending in "one" is feminine (oblique: "-ê").

2. Numbers "two" through "nine" and any multidigital numbers ending in "two" through "nine" are plural (oblique: "-an").

3. The numbers ending in zero: "ten" through "one thousand nine hundred ninety" are declined as masculine (oblique" "-î") even without being modified by the indefinite article or deictics.

4. Even thousands (except 1000, which is included under 3) are declined as plural nouns (oblique: "-an").

 (1) Dest bi yekê bike û bijmêre! - Begin with "one" and count!
 (1) Dest bi bîst û yekê bike û bijmêre! - Begin with 21 and count!
 (1) Dest bi sed û yekê bike û bijmêre! - Begin with 101 and count!
 (1) Dest bi du hezar û yekê û bijmêre! - Begin with 2001 and count!
 (2) Dest bi diduwan bike û bijmêre! - Begin with 2 and count!
 (2) Dest bi sî û sisêyan bike û bijmêre! - Begin with 33 and count!
 (2) Dest bi sed û çaran bike û bijmêre! - Begin with 104 and count!
 (2) Dest bi dehhezar û sed û pêncan bike û bijmêre! - Begin with 10105 and count!
 (3) Dest bi dehî bike û bijmêre! - Begin with 10 and count!
 (3) Dest bi dusedî bike û bijmêre! - Begin with 200 and count!
 (3) Dest bi hezarî bike û bijmêre! - Begin with 1000 and count!
 (4) Dest bi duhezaran bike û bijmêre! - Begin with 2000 and count!
 (4) Dest bi çarhezaran bike û bijmêre! - Begin with 4000 and count!

Exception: the number "one" (yek) will be declined as either masculine or feminine when it is being used in place of a noun, according to the gender of that noun:

 Du zilam hatin; ez niha yekî dibînim. - Two men came; I now see one.
 Du jin hatin; ez niha yekê dibinim. - Two women came; I now see one.

The above rules only apply when the numbers are used as substantives. When a number modifies a noun, the number is not declined and the noun is declined as plural:
 Ez pênc zilaman dibînim. - I see 5 men.

Ez deh zilaman dibînim. - I see 10 men.
Ez bîstûyek zilaman dibînim - I seen 21 men.
Ez hezar zilaman dibînim. - I see 1000 men.
Ez duhezar zilaman dibînim. - I see 2000 men.

9.3 - Ordinal Numbers (ie., first, second, third, etc.)

The ordinal of yek (one) can be made in three different ways.

1. ya pêşî - first
2. yekemîn - the very first
3. ewel or ewelî - first (this form is derived from Arabic)

For the rest of the ordinal numbers, ie, from two on up, one simply adds "an" onto the cardinal numbers, observing spelling rules that require "w" or "y" in certain environments.

diduwan - second
sisêyan - third
çaran - fourth
heftayan - seventieth

Ordinal numbers are treated like adjectives. That is, they are added after the noun by means of the appropriate izafe suffix. This is in contrast to the cardinal numbers which precede the noun they modify.

kitêba diduwan - the second book (du kitêb - two books)
carê pêncan - the fifth time (pênc car - five times)

9.4 - The Comparative & the Superlative

The comparative is formed by adding the suffix "-tir" to the appropriate adjective. The two exceptions to this rule are "pirr" (many, much, very) and "baş" (good). Their respective comparative forms are "bêhtir" and "çêtir". Also, "mezin" (large, great) loses its second syllable when the comparative suffix is added.

pirr (many) » bêhtir (more)
baş (good) » çêtir (better)
mezin (large, great) » meztir (larger, greater)

Kurmanji does not have a superlative as such. To communicate the superlative Kurdish uses the comparative with a phrase like "of (them) all..." or "in the world," etc. (see examples). Sometimes the comparative is not used, the context making it obvious that the superlative is intended.

Kurdistan ji Almanya xweştir e. - Kurdistan is nicer than Germany.
Ew ji min bi quwettir e. - He is stronger than I.
Li dinyayê Kurdistan xweş e. - Kurdistan is the nicest (place) in the world.
Li Kurdistanê Diyarbekir mezin e. - Diyarbakir is the largest (city) in Kurdistan.
Selîm ji hemûwan ciwantir e. - Selim is the youngest of them all.
Bihar ji havîn germtir e? - Is spring hotter than summer?
Na, havîn ji bihar germtir e. - No, summer is hotter than spring.
Zivistan ji hemu demên sartir e. - Winter is the coldest of all the seasons.

comparative statements with "as ... as..."

Azad bi qasî brayê xwe bi quwet e. - Azad is just as strong as his brother.
Azad wek wî zengîn e. - Azad is as rich as he is.
Azad wek wî ne zengîn e. - Azad is not as rich as he is.
Ew ne wek hev in. - They are not the same.

Gotina Xweş - Proverb

Xew ji hesin girantir e, ji sekir şêrîntir e.

Sleep is heavier than iron, sweeter than sugar.

Chapter 10

The Deictics, the Vocative Case and Causatives

10.1 - The Deictics

Deictic words are words one uses to "point out" someone or something which is already known to the speaker and is either close or a bit farther away. In English the deictic words are "this", "that", "these" and "those".

In Kurdish the direct case and the oblique case of the deictic words are quite different. They will be dealt with separately. We have already learned that the direct case deictics are "ev" (this, these) and "ew" (that, those) (see 1.16). Remember that with direct case deictics number and gender are not distinguished and must be understood from other words in the context

The deictics can be used both adjectivally (modifying a noun), or substantively (taking the place of a noun). The deictic forms "evna" and "ewna", which are used with some emphasis to distinguish the intended object from other 3rd person referrants in the context, can only be used substantively.

> Ev kurr jêhatî ye. - This boy is diligent.
> Ev zarok jêhatî ne. - These children are diligent.
> Ew keçik jêhatî ye. - That girl is diligent.
> Ew keçik jêhatî ne. - Those girls are diligent.
> Ev jêhatî ye. - This (one) is diligent.
> Ew jêhatî ye. - That (one) is diligent.
> Ew jêhatî ne. - Those (ones) are diligent.
> Evna jêhatî ne. - These (ones here) are diligent.
> Ewna jêhatî ne. - Those (ones there) are diligent.

10.2 - Oblique Case of the Deictic

The corresponding oblique case deictics do distinguish gender and number. Thus, for every direct case deictic there are three oblique case forms: masculine, feminine and plural. The chart below identifies the different forms of the deictics in the direct and oblique cases.

Direct	Oblique		
	Fem.	*Masc.*	*Plural*
Ev:	vê	vî	van
Ew:	wê	wî	wan
evna:	vêna	vîna	vana
ewna:	wêna	wîna	wana

10.3 - Use of the Oblique Case Deictics

The oblique case deictics can be used both adjectivally and substantively. "Vêna", "vîna", "vana", "wêna", "vîna" and "wana", however, cannot be used adjectivally. They must be used substantively (ie. in place of a noun). Notice that when an oblique case deictic is used adjectivally, the noun receives the appropriate oblique case ending and that ending echoes (rhymes with) the deictic.

> Ez vê (wê) keçikê dibinim. - I see this (that) girl.
> Ez vî (wî) kurrî dibînim. - I see this (that) boy.
> Ez van (wan) zarokan dibînim. - I see these (those) boys.
> Ez vê dibînim. - I see this one (fem.).
> Ez wêna dibînim. - I see that one there (fem.).
> Ez wana dibînim - I see those ones there.

10.4 - The Deictic Word "Ha" - this here, these here

"Ha" is used to intensify "ev" and "ew". It is bound to the preceding noun or deictic by izafe. It is used somewhat like people from the southern USA say, "this here...". Speakers who use this form do not usually use the emphatic deictics (evna, ewna, etc.).

> Ev keça ha jehatî ye. - This here girl is diligent. (or, This girl here is diligent.)
> Ev kurrê ha jehatî ye. - This here boy is diligent. (or, This boy here is diligent.)
> Ev zarokên ha jehatî ne. - These here children are diligent, (or,

These children here are diligent.)
eva ha - this one here (fem.)
evê ha - this one here (masc.)
evên ha - these here
ewa ha - that one (fem.)
ewê ha - that one (masc.)
ewên ha - those ones

10.5 - Vocatives

Vocatives denote someone or something which is addressed or called. English vocatives might be "Hey!", or "Hey you!" In Kurmanji the vocative is much more common than in English. The vocative is formed by adding certain endings to the name or noun addressed. The endings differ according to whether the addressee is masculine, feminine, or plural.

Fem. vocative ending: "-ê"
Masc. vocative ending: "-o"
Plural vocative ending: "-no"

Keçê! - O girl / Hey, girl!
Kurro! - O boy / Hey, boy!
Keçno! - O girls / Hey, girls!
Kurrno! - O boys / Hey, boys!
Xalo / amo! - O uncle / Hey, uncle!
Xaltikê! - O aunt / Hey aunt!
Rebenê! - Poor thing (fem.)!
Rebeno! - Poor thing (masc.)!
Kero! - You, donkey!
Lingê te saqeto! - You with the lame leg!

Vocatives are strengthened by the optional addition of a particle "lê" for feminine, "lo" for masculine or plural. These particles precede the noun with the vocative ending. They are frequently used in love songs, setting off the alternating male and female parts:

Lo Kurro! - Hey boy!
Lê Keçê! - Hey girl!
Lo Kurrno! - Hey boys!
Lo Keçno! - Hey girls!

55

10.6 - Vocative and Proper Names

There are two ways to put proper names into the vocative. The appropriate vocative ending can be added to the proper name. The stress will fall on the penultimate syllable. Or, no vocative ending is added; instead, the proper name becomes stressed on the first syllable. Some names already end in "-o" or "-ê" without the vocative case. For vocative use the stress again shifts forward.

> Azad » **Azad**o or **Az**ad!
> Sînem » **Sînem**ê or **Sî**nem!
> Silo » **Si**lo!

10.7 - Vocative and Social Status

You might find that some men's names have feminine endings and some women's names masculine endings. The reason for this is that sometimes the masculine vocative "-o" is used for a "non-noble" social class, and the feminine vocative ending "-ê" is used for the noble, aristocratic class. Thus, the agha's son might be called "Bubê!", while "Bubo!" would be for the farmers son. "Xeçê!" might be used for the nobleman's daughter, "Xeço!" for the peasant's girl.

10.8 - Causatives

Causatives are a category of transitive verbs. They are verbs of action by which an effect is produced. Many intransitive verbs can be made into causative transitive verbs (ie., My hand burns » Something burns my hand).

To form the causative in Kurmanji you take the present stem of the intransitive verb and add the suffix "andin". The endings "îne" or alternatively, "êne" are the corresponding endings for the imperative (2nd dictionary) form of causatives. To form the causative imperative simply add these endings and prefix "bi-" to the intransitive (past tense) stem.

Note: The intransitive verb and its causative form will be two different listings in the dictionary.

> şewitîn, bişewite - to bum » şewit + andin = şewitandin, bişewitîne - to cause something to burn, burn (that)!

çêrîn, biçêre - to graze » çêrandin, biçêrîne - to take to pasture
tirsîn, bitirse - to be afraid » tirsandin, bitirsîne - to scare, to
frighten
Wî ez tirsandim - He scared me.

Sometimes the causative will have a more selective meaning than the intransitive verb to which it is related:

mirin, bimre - to die » mirandin, bimrîne - to extinguish, to turn off (but not "to kill").

10.9 - The Causative with Foreign Words

The causative is often used to build verbs out of foreign stems imported into Kurdish.

belifandin, bibelifîne - to fool, to cause someone to be fooled
(comes from the English verb "to bluff).

10.10 - Causative of "bûn, bibe" (to be, to become): kirin, bike

The causative of a compound with "bûn, bibe (to be)" is the corresponding compound with "kirin, bike" (to make, to do, to cause to become)

Ez gêj bûm. - I became dizzy.
Wî ez gêj kirim. - He made me dizzy.

10.11 - " Hiştin, bihêle" (to let, to allow, to cause) and the Causative

When the verb "hiştin, bihêle" is used with a subordinate, the subordinate clause begins with "ku" (that, which, who). The verb in the subordinate clause must be in the subjunctive. "Ku" (that, which, who) can be dropped without changing the meaning of the sentence. It is then understood from the context. The verb of the subordinate clause remains in the subjunctive even if the "ku" is dropped.

Ez nahêlim ku ew raze. - I don't allow him to sleep (I don't allow that he sleep).
Min hişt ku ew werre ba we. - I allowed (that) him to come to you.
Ba dihêle ku agir zû vede. - Wind causes (that) the fire to light quickly.
Ba dihêle agir zû vede. - Wind causes the fire to light quickly.

10.12 - "Dan, bide" (to give) and the Causative

Normally "dan, bide" means "to give". However, it can also mean "to cause" when an infinitive is used after it. In a negative sentence "dan, bide" can mean "to not allow, to not let, to cause not to". The sense of the accompanying infinitive is normally passive.

> Ez wê didim xwendin. - I cause it (fem.) to be read.
> Ez wî didim naskirin. - I cause him to be known (ie. I introduce him).
> Ew karkeran nadin karkirin. - He didn't let the workers work.
> Ew beşê dîrokê bi kurrê xwe dide xwendin. - He teaches (causes to be read) the subject of history to his son. (Note the preposition"bi" to introduce the indirect object).

10.13 - Exceptions to Causative Rules

A small number of verbs correspond to each other in meaning but not in form; ie, they mean almost the same thing, but one is transitive and causetive while the other is intransitive. These verbs have to be learned as separate verbs.

Intrans. Verb	Trans. Verb
hatin, were - to come	anîn, bîne - to bring, to cause to come
ketin, bikeve - to fall	xistin, bixe - to cause to fall, to throw, to put in

Gotina Xweş - Proverb

Zikê bixwe savarê, divê herre hawarê

Stomach that eats bulgar, it must go help.

(If you have eaten in someone's house,
you must also go to the help of that household.)

Chapter 11

Prepositions, Postpositions
and Conjuntions

11.1 - Prepositions and Postpositions

Kurdish prepositions are often complemented by a postposition. In order to get the true shade of meaning intended by the preposition it is often, though not always, necessary to place this postposition after the object of the preposition.

It is possible to have a preposition without a postposition. In fact some prepositions never occur with a postposition. But, depending on the dialect, you almost never have a postposition without a preposition. It is easiest to think of postpositions as extensions of the preposition.

The postpositions are as follows:

> ... de
> ... re
> ... ve

Although attempts have been made to impose certain shades of meaning on the postpositions, one can always find exceptions to the rule. However, in very general terms it might be possible to say that:

> "... de" incorporates the idea of inclusion, containing, comprising;
>
> "... re" incorporates the idea of accompaniment, companionship, a being along with;
>
> "... ve" incorporates the idea of movement (both spacially: "where to, on" and temporally: "since when...", as well as the idea of accompaniment).

11.2 - Prepositions and Different Postposition Combinations

ba - to, towards; beside, with
> Emê sibê bên ba we. - Tomorrow we will come to you.
> Havînan li Ingilizstanê ne weke ba me germ e. - Summers are not as warm in England as with us.

ber - in front of
> Hêk deyne ber goştê. - Put the egg in front of the meat.

berbi - straight towards, against
> Ew berbi min tê. - He's coming straight towards me. He's coming against me.

be - without
> Bê te em nikarin dest bi nimêj bikin. - We cannot begin our prayers without you.

bi - with, by means of ("bi" can also be used to introduce indirect objects)
> "Xwedê hertiştê ku çêkiribû dit û bi wan pirr kêfxweş bû" (Kitêba Musa ya Pêşî 1:31). - God saw everything he had made and with it was very happy (Gen. 1:31).
> Ew beşê dîrokê bi kurrê xwe dide xwendin. - He teaches (causes to be read) the subject of history to his son.

bi ... re - with, along with
> Ew bi min re dimîne. - He stays with me.

bi ... ve - together with, on
> Mirov bi jinê ve dikene. - The man is laughing together with the woman.

di ... ve - through
> Emê di Stambolê ve biçin Ankarayê. - We will travel through Istanbul en route to Ankara.

di ... de - in, inside
> "Xwedê di destpêkê de erd û ezman avakirin" (Kitêba Musa ya Peşî 1:1). - "In the beginning God created earth and heaven" (Gen. 1:1).

di ... re - by, via
> Emê di Ankarê re biçin Stambolê. - We are going to travel to Istanbul via Ankara.

dibin ... de - under, underneath (when subject is not moving)
Kitêb dibin maseyê de ye. - The book is under the table.

dibin ... re - under, underneath (when subject is moving)
Keştî dibin pirê re diçe. - The ship is going under the bridge.

dinav ... de - in the middle, among
Mala min dinav daristanê de ye. - My house is in the middle of the forest.
Dinav Kurdan de yek zû hînî zimanê Kurdî dibe. - Among the Kurds one learns Kurdish quickly.

dinav ... re - through (when subject is moving)
Em her sibe dinav daristanê re diçîn. - Every morning we go through the forest

diser ... re - on, over (for both moving and immobile subjects)
Lempe diser masê re ye. - The lamp is on the table.
Ew diser pirê re diçin. - They are going over the bridge.

heya, heta, ta, heya bi - until, as far as
Ez heya Stambolê diçim. - I'm going as far as Istanbul.
Heya bi Stambolê 8 seet in. - It's 8 hours until Istanbul.

ji - from, out of
Ew ji xwendegehê tê. - He's coming from school.
Ew jin penêr ji şîr çêdike. - This woman is making cheese from milk.
Ew ji tirsan naçe wê derê. - Out of fear(s) he doesn't go there.

ji ... ve - from; as of, since
Ew ji sibehî ve digrî. - He has been crying since morning [lit. is crying].
Ew ji vê gundê ve tê. - He comes from that village.

ji ... re - to, for
Şikir ji Xwedê re. - Thanks be to God.

li - in (a place, thing); for, about (when used with verbs "gerin" and "pirsin")
Wek İsa tu kes nine, ne li erdê, ne jî li ezmên. - Like Jesus there is no one, not in the earth nor in the heavens.
Ez li vî digerim. - I'm looking for him (this one).

61

Ew li vî dipirse. - he's asking about him (this one).

li pey - after, behind (with motion)
Îsa got: "Ez rê me. Li pey min werrin". - Jesus said: "I am the way. Come after me".

li gora - according to
"Tiştên ku li ser axê şilo dibin, li gora babetê wan derxe" (K. Musa ya Peşin 1:24). - "(All) things that move upon the soil, produce according to their sort" (Gen. 1:24).

liser - on, above, about
"Rûhê Xwedê liser avê vegerriya" (K. Musa ya Pesi 1:1). - "The Spirit of God above the water was wandering" (Gen. 1:1).
Tu çi dibêjî liser van tiştan? - What do you have to say about these things?

rex - beside
Here rex diya xwe. - Go beside your mother.

ser - on, to
kitêban deyne ser masê - Put the books on the table
Emê diçın ser Stambolê. - We are going to Istanbul.

11.3 - Conjuctions

Conjunctions are never conjugated and have no case.

(bi) tenê, bes - only, except
Em hemû çûn malê, (bi)tenê Memo li xwendegehê ma bû. - We all went home, only Memo remained at school.

bila - also, even if (lit. let, granted that, allowing that)
Bila rê dûr be jî, ewê be. - Even if the road is long, he will come.

çi ... çi ... - whether... or whether
Şêr şer e, çi jin e çi mêr e. - A lion a lion is whether it is female or whether it is male.

çima ku, jiber ku - because, on account of
"Lê layiq bû ku em şa û geş bibin, çima ku ev brayê te mirî bû, û sax bû; winda bû, û hate dîtin" (Luqa 15:32). - "But we had to celebrate and be glad, because this brother of yours was dead and

is alive again; he was lost and is found" (Luke 15:32).
Jiber ku ez dixwazim bi Kurdî bihalimim, ez tim bi Kurdî
dixwînim. - Because I want to learn Kurdish I always read
Kurdish.

dajiboy, jibona (ku) - in order to
"Mesîh hatiye dinyayê jibona ku gunehkaran xelas bike" (1 Tim.
1:15). - "Christ came into the world in order to save sinners" (1
Tim. 1:15).

gelo - whether (also used as an interrogative particle, introducing a question)
Ez nizanim gelo ew rehat e yan na. - I don't know whether he is
comfortable or not.
Gelo bavê wî hê can e? - Is his father still living?

jiber vê yekê, ji ber wê yekê, ji ber wilo - therefore, on account of
this/that, for this reason
Ew nehat. Jiber vê yekê ez çûm. - He didn't come. For this reason I
left.

jî - also, too (sometimes used where we use "and" in English. It is used
after the word it modifies.)
Ez jî başim. - I am also fine.
Tû jî çawa yî? - And how are you?

...jî û ... jî - as well as, **hem ... hem** - as well as, **hem ... (jî), hem... jî** -
both ... and
Li Elmanya baran havînan jî û zivistanan jî tê. - In Germany it
rains in the summers as well as in the winters (lit. rain comes).
Li Elmanya baran hem havînan hem zivistanan jî tê. - In Germany
it rains both in summer and in the winter.
Hem rêvî (jî), hem gur jî hene. - There are both foxes and wolves.

ku (ko, go, dialectal variants) - that, which, whose (technically not a
conjunction but a relative pronoun)
Heviya min ew e, ku tu vegerrî. - My hope it is, that you come.
Min dît ku gotinên wî rast e. - I saw that his words were the truth.
Ez zanim ku ewê sibe be. - I know that he will come tomorrow.

lê - but
Em tamam însan in lê em bi zimanê hev fehm nakin. - We are all
people but we don't understand the same language.

lêbelê - on the other hand, (a strong "but")

"Ez ronahiya dinyayê me; yê ku li pey min bê ew di reşiyê de qet nameşe, lêbelê ronahiya wê ya hayatê wê hebe." (Yuh. 8:12). - I am the light of the world; whoever follows me is not at all walking in darkness, but will have the light of life" (John 8:12).

ne ... ne ... jî - neither... nor...

Tu kesê wek İsa nine, ne li erdê, ne jî li ezman. - There is nobody like Jesus, neither on earth nor in heaven.

û - and (many couples coupled by "û" are treated as one grammatically. The word with the least letters usually comes first.)

ez û tu - I and you (note: 1st person comes first)
tîr û kevan - arrow and bow
Min tîr û kevan dît. - I saw an arrow and bow. (dît is singular)
çep û rast - left and right
nan û mast - bread and yoghurt

Often a string of clauses which share a common subject and depict a sequence of events can be juxtaposed one after the other without the use of a conjunction and without repeating the subject. Note the absence of "û" where in English we would use "and":

Rabû çû, bi çolê ket û li xwarinê geriye. - He got up (and) went, he got to (lit. fell) the desert and looked for food.

wilo ... ku ... - so... that...

Dinya wilo germ bû ku mirov nikarî bû derkeve ji derve. - The weather was so warm, people could not go outside.

ya(n), an (dialectal variants) - or

subhê yan dusbê ezê bêm. - I will come tomorrow or the day after.

ya(n) ... ya(n) jî - either... or

Ew ya li malê, ya li xwendegehê ye. - He is either at home or at school.

yanî - for example, in other words, meaning, that is

Ev sahat xerab bû, yani, skestî bû. - This watch went bad, that is, it was broken.

11.4 - Temporal conjuntions

berî ku - before

Berî ku tu nehatî bû Elmanya te nezanî bû bi Kurdi. - Before you
had (not) come to Germany you didn't know Kurdish. (Before
coming to Germany you didn't know Kurdish.)

dema ku, gava ku, wextê ku, çaxê ku - when

Dema ku ez têm mal, diya min cilan dişo. - When I come home my
mother washes the clothes.

Gava ku ez têm mal ez tim kitêban dixwînim. - When I come
home I always read books.

Çaxê ku ez li mal bim carna ez yaziyê dinivisim. - When I am at
home I sometimes write (writing).

Wextê ku ez li mal bim hevalên min tên, gelekî kefa min tê. - The
time that (when) I am at home, my friends come, I am very
pleased (lit. my pleasure comes).

di çaxê ku - while

Di çaxê ku ew kitêba dixwînê diya wi (jê) cilan dişo. - While he is
reading a book, his mother is washing the clothes.

eger, heke, go - if (conditional), when (temporal).

Eger ew baştir nebe, dive em wî bibin textor. - If he doesn't
become better, we must take him to the doctor.

Heke pirsa wan hebe, ber niha bêjin. - If they have a question, let
them speak now.

Heke tu hatî emê tevde çayekê vexwin. - When you come we will
drink tea together, (perfective aspect in subordinate clause for a
definite future. Thus "heke" translates best as "when", and is thus
temporal rather than conditional.

hema, heme ku - as soon as, immediatly

Hema ku bêm mal ezê telefonê ji te re vekim. - As soon as I come
home I will telephone you.

beta, heya, ta - until

Heta tu doceh (cehenemê) nabînê, buheşt bi te xweş nabê. - You
cannot appreciate heaven until you have seen hell.

hingî - then

Pêşî wî xaniyê xwe firot, hingî wî dixwest vî disa bikirre. - First he
sold his house then he wanted to buy it back.

ji çaxê ku - since, from the time that...

Ji çaxê ku bûye havîn me hê du heftan germ nedîne. - Since it became summer we still haven't seen two warm weeks.

pistî ku - after (pistre - afterwards)
Pistî ku min dît ew hevalê qenc bû kêfa min gelekî jê hat. - After I saw that he was a good friend, I was very pleased with him (lit. my pleasure much came from him).
Pistî du salan ew rehmet çû. - After two years he died (lit. mercy went).

pêşî - first, firstly
Pêşî wî xaniyê xwe firot. - First he sold his house.

Gotina Xweş - Proverb

Destê bi tenê deng jê nayê

One hand by itself (ie. a one handed clap) makes no sound.

Chapter 12

Quantifiers and Question Words

12.1 - Quantifiers

Quantifiers are adverbs that show the amount of something. If the long list of quantifiers below looks threatening, remember that not every dialect uses all of them! Listen for and learn the ones you hear spoken by the people around you. Eventually learn to recognize the other ones as well.

çend - some (see also 12:2)
> Ez çend kitêban dixwazim. -1 want some books (kitêban is in the plural oblique).
> Çend xwendekar hatin. - Some students came (xwendekar is plural but in direct case).

çendek - some
> Çendek hatin, çendek çûn. - Some came and some went.
> "Lê çendek ji wan gotin: Ew bi Balzebûlî, serekê dêwan, dêw dertîne" (Luqa 11:15) - "But some of them said, 'By Beelzebub, the prince of demons, he is driving out demons'" (Luke 11:15).

çiqa(s) - how much, so much (for noncount nouns. See also 12:2)
> "Bavê we yê ezmanî çiqas bêtir wê Rûhê Paqij bide yên ku ji wî dixwazin? (Luqa 11.13). - "How much more will your heavenly father give the Holy Spirit to those who ask him (Luke 11:13).
> Bindest bûn çiqa zor e! - Being oppressed is so hard!
> Wî çiqa şekir anî! - How much sugar he brought!

din, dî (dialectal variants) - other, else
> Ez bajarna din nasdikim. -1 know some other cities.
> Tiştekî dî jî heye. - There is something else, too.

gelek, pirr, zehf - many (can be used adjectivally and pronominally)
> Gelek zarok diçin vê xwendegehê. - Many children go to that school.

Gelek diçin vê xwendegehê - Many go to that school.

Ez pirr xwendekaran nasdikim. - I know many students.

Zehf Kurd li Elmanya hene. - There are many Kurds in Germany.

heçî, herkî - whoever, everyone

Heçiyê ku bi me re werre, bere destê xwe hilde. - Whoever is coming with us (let him) raise his hand.

Heçiyê ku tu wê nasdikî, şanî me bike. - Everyone who knows him, show me.

"Herkî ku dixwaze distîne" (Luqa 11:10) - "Everyone who wants receives" (Luke 11:10).

hemû, hemî, gişk, giş, gi - all, everything, everyone.

"Werrne ba min, hun hemî ku kardikin û dilteng in! Ezê rehatî bidem we" (Matta 11:28). - "Come unto me all you who labour and are heavy laden, and I will give you rest" (Mat. 11:28).

her - every, each

Min ev her car nedî. - I didn't see him (this one) every time.

herkes, heryek - everybody, everyone

Herkes karê vî karî bike? - Can everybody do this job?

hertişt - everything

"û gelek wext ne borî, kurrê piçûk hertişt da hev û çû welatekî dûr, û li wê bi tolazî malê xwe telef kir" (Luqa 15:13). - "Not long after that, the younger son got together all he had, set off for a distant country and there squandered his wealth in wild living" (Luke 15:13).

hin, hinek - some, a few, a number, many

Hin heval diçin kardikin. - Some friends are going and working.

Ez hinan ji wan nasnakim. - I don't know some of them.

hîç - none ... at all, no... at all, none, nothing (always negative)

Hîç xeber ji te re ji wan nehatine? - Has any news for you arrived at all from them?

kes, kesek, tukes - anybody, anyone, nobody, no one

Tu kesek wek İsa Mesih ne li erdê ne jî li ezman tune. - There is nobody in heaven or on earth like Jesus Christ.

kêm, hindik (dialectal variants) - a little (bit)

Ez Kurmanji hindik zanim. - I know Kurmanji a little bit.

tim - always
Xwedê tim gotina xwe dibe serî. - God always makes his word succeed.

tiştek - a thing, something, or with negative verbs: nothing, not anything.
Tiştek ji te re ji wan hatiye. - Something has come for you from them.
Ez tiştekî ji we nabînim. - I am not seeing anything of you.

tu - not any, none, nothing at all
Tu tişt nine. - It is nothing at all.
"Tu însan tu caran weke wî zilamî xeber neda" (Yuh. 7:46). - "Not any person not any time has (not) spoken (given words) like this man" (John 7:46).

yek - somebody, someone, one
"Yan kî ye ew jina ku deh dînarên wê hebe û ku yekî ji wan winda bike, çirayê vênexe ku malê gêzê bike û bi miqateyî lê bigere heta wî bibîne?" (Luqa 15:8) - "Or suppose a woman has ten silver coins (dinars) and loses one. Does she not light a lamp, sweep the house and search carefully until she finds it?" (Luke 15:8).

12.2 - Question Words

Question words are words like who, what, when, where, which, how, etc. which form the basis for questions. Notice that some of them also occur as quantifiers (see sec. 12.1).

çawa & çilo - how
Tu çawa yî? - How are you?
Tu çilo kurrê xwe bibînî? - How will you find your son?

çend - how many (used with "count" nouns. See also 12.1)
Çend hene? - How many are there?
Çend qelem hene? - How many pens are there?
Tu çend kitêban dixwazî? - How many books do you want?
Tu çendan dixwazî? - How many do you want? (note plural oblique case, as though "çend" were a noun)

çi - what (if "çi" is followed by a noun it means "what kind of" or "what sort of")

> Ew çi kitêban dixwînin? - What kind of books are they reading?
> Wî çi got? - What did he say?
> Tu di heqê Îsa Mesîh de çi bawer dikî? - What do you believe
> about Jesus Christ?

çi wext - what time

> Tu çi wext hatî? - What time did you come?

çima - why

> Tu çima hatî? - Why did you come?
> "Îsa bi dengekî bilind digot, 'Elî, Elî, lama sebeqtanî?' Yani,
> Xwedayê min, Xwedayê min, te çima ez terk kirim?" (Matta
> 27:46) - "Jesus cried out with a loud voice, "Eli Eli lama
> sabaxtani', that is, 'My God, my God, why have you left me?'"

çiqa(s) - how much (with noncount nouns. See also 12.1), **ciqasî** - how
(long)

> Çiqas şêr heye? - How much milk is there?
> Çiqa cay ez bikirrim? - How much tea should I buy?
> Çiqasî dûr e? - How far is it?
> Tu çiqasî diminî - How long are you staying?

çira - why, what for

> Wê çira ev kiriye? - Why has she done this?

gelo, ma - interrogative particle, "Is it so that...?" "Gelo" normally
introduces real questions while "ma" introduces rhetorical questions.

> Gelo zarokê wan hene? - Do they have children?
> Ma tiştek heye ku Xwedê nikare? - Is there anything that God can't
> do?

ji kuderê - from where

> Tu ji kuderê hatî? - Where do you come from?

kengî - when

> Tu kengî hatî? - When did you come?

kî - who (in oblique case, "kê"; but in some dialects only one or the other
will be used regardless of case.)

> Kî hat cem we? - Who came to your place?
> Kê ez dîtim? - Who saw me?
> "Lewra her kî ku xwe bilind dike wê nizm bibe, û kî ku xwe nizm
> dike wê bête bilindkirin (Luqa 14:11). - "Because everyone who

70

exalts himself will be brought low, and whoever lowers himself will be lifted up" (Luke 14:8).

kîjan (kujan) - which (of them) (Can be used alone or with a noun)
    Kîjan çêtir e? - Which one is better?
    Kîjan kitêb çêtir e? - Which book is better?
    Tu kîjanê (in fem. oblique if its object is fem.) dixwazî?- Which one do you want? (object of "one" must be feminine).
    Tu kîjanî dixwazî (kîjan is masc. if its object is masc.) - Which one do you want?
    Tu kîjan keçê nasdikî? - Which girl do you know?
    Tu kîjanan dixwazî? - Which ones do you want? (note plural oblique marker "kîjan-an")
    Tu kîjan kurran dîbînî? - Which boys do you see?

Kuderê - where (lit. which place)
    Ew diçe kuderê? - Where is he going?

Li kuderê - in, where
    Ew li kuderê dimîne? - Where does he live?

Gotina Xweş - Proverb

Riya dûr çêtir e ji tirba kûr.

A long road is better than a deep grave.

Vocabulary

A.

adetî - normal

afir (m.) - manger

agir (m.) - fire

ajotin, bajo! - to drive

alî (m.) - side, area, direction

alîkarî kirin - to help

Almanya - Germany

amo (m.) - uncle

an - or

anişk (f.) - forehead

anîn, bîne! - to bring, to cause to come

av (f.) - water

av dan - to water (plants)

ava bûn - to thrive, to increase

ava kirin - to cause to prosper

avêtin, bavêje! - to throw, to fire (weapon)

avis - pregnant (for animals)

axa (m.) - agha

axiftin, baxive! - to speak

azad - free

azadî (f.) - freedom

B.

ba (m.) - wind, rheumatism

ba - to, towards, as, at

bablîsok (f.)- wind swirl, gust of wind

bajar (m.) - city

bajarî - city dweller

bajêr (m.) - city (oblique case)

bav (m.) - father

bawer kirin - to believe

bawî - rheumatic

baş - good

began (m.) - lords

behtir - more

belek - speckled, spotted, striped, having mixed colours

ber - in front of

berbi - straight towards, against

berî - before

bersîv / bersiv (f.) - answer

berx (m.) - lamb

bes - except, only, just

beş (f.) - share, part, subject

bê - without

bêrî (f.) - pining, homesickness; milkmaid

bêş (f.) - tax, fine

bêvil (f.) - nose

bi - with, by means of

bi ... re - with, along with

bi ... ve - together with, on

bi aqil - intelligent

bi çi - with what

bi qasî - by the amount of

bi tenê - only, alone

biçûk - small

bihar (f.) - spring

bihn (f.) - smell

bila - even if, allowing that

bilind - high

bindest kirin - to subjugate

birastî - in truth

bircî - hungry

bircîtî (f.) - hunger

bîst - twenty

bîr (f.) - well; memory, mind

boz - grey

C.

car (f.) - time (as in "2nd time")

cejn (f.) - feast

cem - to, towards

cih (m.) - place

cil (pl.) - clothes

cins (m.) - lineage, sex, type

civîn, bicive! - to meet together

ciwan - young

cotkar (m.) - farmer

Ç.

ça (f.) - tea

çar - four

çaran - fourth

çarde - fourteen

çav (m.) - eye

çawa - how

çaxê ku - when

çay (f.) - tea

çêbûn, çêbibe! - to succeed, to be born, to heal, to grow, to mature

çekdar - armed

çêkirin - to make, to fix, to repair, to prepare (a meal)

çend - how many, how much, several, some

çendek - some

çerandin, biçêrîne! - to put out to pasture, cause to graze.

çetir - better

çêrîn, biçêre! - to graze

çi - what, what kind of

çi ... çi - whether... whether

çil - forty

çilo - how

çima - why

çiqa, çiqas - how much, how very

çirav (f.) - mud, muck; marsh, swamp

çûn, biçe / herre! - to go

D.

dagirtin, dagre! - to fill

dagirkirin - to occupy

dajiboy - in order to

daketin, dakeve! - to come down, to descend

dan, bide! - to give

deh - ten

dem (f.) - time, season

dema ku - when

deranîn, derîne! - to take out

derbas bûn - to pass, to enter

derd (m.) - hardship, ache, sorrow

derew (m.) - lie

dergevan (m./f.) - door-keeper, guard

dergistî - engaged, betrothed

derî (m.) - door

derketin, derkeve! - to leave, to set out

derman (m.) - medicine

deşt (f.) - prairie, plain

dev (m.) - mouth

dew (m.) - watered down yoghurt, buttermilk

dewar (m.) - cattle, animals

di ... de - in, inside

di heqa ... de - about, concerning

di ... re - by, via

di ... ve - through

di çaxê ku - while

dibin ... de - under, underneath (when the subject is not moving)

dibin ... re - under, underneath (when the subject is moving)

didu - two

diduwan - second

digel - with

dijmin (m./f.) - enemy

dil (m.) - heart

dilop (f.) - drop (of liquid)

dilovan - tender, merciful

din - other

dinav ... de - in the middle, among

dinav ... re - through

dinya (f.) - world, weather

dirêj - long, tall

dirêjayî (f.) - length

diser ... re - on

divê - should, ought to

dî - other

dîrok (f.) - history

dîsa - again

dîtin, bibîne! - to see

doh - yesterday

dora - around

dost (m./f.) - friend, lover

du, do - two (followed by noun)

dua kirin - to pray

duh - yesterday

dupişk - scorpion

duwandzde - twelve

dû (f.) - smoke

dûr - far

dûrayî (f.) - distance

E.

ecêbmayî - amazed

efu (f.) - forgiveness

efu kirin - to forgive

eger - if

em - we, us

emir (m.) - command; age

emir kirin - to command

erd (f.) - earth, land

ev - this, these

evna - this (one), this here, these (ones), these here

ew - that/those, they/them, he/she/it

ewel - first

ewelî - first

ewna - that (one), that there, those (ones), those there

ez - I, me

ezman (m.) - heaven

F.

feqîr - poor, nice

ferman (f.) - decree

ferman kirin - to issue a decree

firotin, bifroşe! - to sell

firrîn, bifirre! - to fly

G.

gava ku - when

gelek - many, very

gelo - whether, interogative particle

gemar - dirty

gerek - should, ought to

gerek bûn - to be necessary

germ - warm

germayî (f.) - warmth

gerş - dirty

gi - all, everything

gindirîn, bigindire! - to roll, to tumble

giran - heavy

girêdan, girêde! - to tie

giring - important

girî (f.) - crying

girîn, bigrî! - to cry, to weep

girtin, bigre! - to catch, to close

gişk - all, everything

go - that, which, whose, if

gotin, (bi)beje! - to say

gotina xweş - proverb

gotinên peşiya - proverbs, sayings of the teachers

goşt (m.) - meat

guh dan, guh bide! - to give ear to, to listen

gund (m.) - village

gundî (m./f.) - villager

guneh (m.) - sin

guneh kirin - to sin

H.

hakim (m.) - judge

hakîm (m.) - healer, traditional doctor

hatin, were! - to come

havîn (f.) - summer

hawar (f.) - help, aid

hawîr - among

hawîrdora - surrounding

hayat - life

hazir bûn - to be prepared, ready

hazir kirin - to prepare

hebûn, hebe! - to exist

heçî - whoever, all

heft - seven

hefta - seventy

heftayan - seventieth

hejar - poor

hejarî (f.) - poverty

heke - if

hem ... hem - both ... and ...

hema - as soon as, immediately

hemd (f.) - praise

hemeku - as soon as, immediately

hemî - all, everything

hemû - all, everything

hene - see hebûn

her - every

herkes - everybody

hertişt - everything

heryek - everyone

hesin (m.) - iron

hesinî - made of iron, ironlike

heşt - eight

heşta - eighty

heta - until, as far as

heta heta - forever

heval (m./f.) - friend

hewce - necessary

heya - until, as far as

heye - see hebûn

hezar - one thousand

hêk (f.) - egg

hêlîn (f.) - nest

hîç - none... at all, no ... at all, none, nothing

hijde (m.) - eighteen

hildan, hilde! - to raise, to lift

hin - some, a few, a number

hindik - a little

hinek -some, a few, a number

hingî - then (temporal or logical)

hirç (f.) - bear

hiş - consciousness, reason

hivde (m.) - seventeen

hiştin, bihêle! - to let, to allow

hîn bûn - to learn

hîn kirin - to teach

hun - you (pl.)

I.

Incîl - gospel

Î.

îro - today

îsa (m.) - Jesus

J.

jan (f.) - pain, ache

jana zirav - tuberculosis

jêhatî - diligent, industrious

ji - from, than, out of

ji ... re - for, to

ji ... ve - from, as of, since

ji ber çi - because of what, why

ji ber ku (jiber ku) - because, on account of

ji çaxê ko - since, from the time that

ji kuderê - from where

jiber ve yekê - for this reason

jiber wilo - for this reason

jibona - in order to

jimardin, bijmêre! - to count

jin (f.) - woman

jinişkave - suddenly

jî - also, too

... jî û ... jî -... as well as...

jîn, bijî! - to live

jîyandin, bijîne! - to cause to live, to quicken, to enliven

K.

kamil - perfect, complete

karîn, bikare! - to be able to

karker (m./f.) - worker

karkirin - to work

Karkirinê Şagirtiyan - Acts of the Apostles

keç (f.) - girl, daughter

keçel - bald

keçik (f.) - little girl, daughter

kelpîç (m.) - brick

ken (f.) - laughter, smile

kengî - when

kenîn, bikene! - to laugh

ker (m.) - donkey

kes - anybody, anyone, person; nobody, no one, with neg. verb

kesek - anybody, anyone; nobody, no one, with neg. verb

kesk - green, green-blue

ketin, bikeve! - to fall

ketî - falling

kevir (m.) - stone

keyfxweş - joyful

keyfxwesî (f.) - joy

kê - who

kêm - little (amount)

kin - short

kiras (m.) - shirt

kirin, bike! - to do, to make

kirîv (m./f.) - godparent

kirîvatî (f.) - godparenthood

kirrîn, bikirre! - to buy

kitêb (f.) - book

Kitêba Muqedes - Bible

kî - who

kîjan - which

ko - that, which, whose

kor - blind

koz (f.) - cinder

ku - that, which, whose

kuderê - where

kuflet (f.)-child

kurr (m.) - boy, son

kurrik (m.) little boy, son

Kurdistan (f.) - Kurdistan

kuştin, bikuje! - to kill, to murder

kun (f.) - cut, hole

kûjan - which

kûr - deep

kûrayî (f.) - depth

L.

lazim - must, necessary

lewra - therefore

leşker (m.) - soldier

lê - but

lêbelê - on the other hand, but

lêxisitin, bileyize! - to hit, to throw; to play a musical instrument

li - in

78

li gora - according to

li kuderê - in, where

ling (m.) - leg

liser - on, about

livîn, bilive! - to move (intransitive)

M.

ma - interogative particle

ma gelo - interogative particle

ma wilo - interogative particle

mayî - remaining (lit: remained)

mal (f.) - home, household; possessions; family

maldar - rich

mamoste (m./f.) - teacher

man, bimîne! - to stay, to remain

masî (m.) - fish

mast (m.) - yoghurt

me - we, us, ours

mecbûr - definitely must

melek (m.) - angel

merg (m.) - death

Mesîh (m.) - Christ

meydan (f.) - plaza, square

mezin - large, great

meztir - larger, greater

mêr (m.) - man; brave

mêranî (f.) - manliness, bravery

mêrkuj - bloodthirsty

mêş (f.) - fly (insect)

mêvan (m./f.) - guest

mih (f.) - sheep, ewe

mihim - important (also muhim & mihum)

mila (m.) - mullah

milet (m.) - people, ethnic group

min - I, me, mine

mirandin, bimrîne! - to turn off, to extinguish

mirin, bimre! - to die

mirov (m.) - person, man

mirovatî (f.) - humanity, humanness

mizgîn (m.) - good news

mîr (m.) - prince

mû (m.) - hair (single hair; see also porr)

N.

nalîn, binale! - to wail, to lament

nan (m.) - bread

naskirin - to be acquainted, to know

nav (m.) - middle

ne ... ne ... - neither... nor...

neh - nine

nexweş - sick, unpleasant

nexweşî (f.) - sickness, disease

nêzik - near

niha - now

nimêj kirin - to pray

nivîsandin, binivîse! - to write

nivîsîn, binivîse! - to write

nizim - low

nîne - there isn't (any) (see hebun)

nînin - there aren't (any) (see hebun)

nîvisk (m.) - butter

nîşan (f.) - sign, symbol, mark

not - ninety

nozde - nineteen

O.

ode (f.) - room

P.

panzde - fifteen

parmend - joy, enjoyment

pencî - fifty

penîr (f.) - cheese

pez (m.) - sheep

pênc - five

pêşî (f.) - flea

pêşî - front, prior

pêxember (m.) - prophet

pêxistin, pêxe! - to light, to ignite, to turn on

pirr - very, many, much

pirranî (f.) - the majority

pirs (f.) - question, problem

piştî ku - after

pistre - afterwards

pîrek (f.) - woman, wife

pîroz - holy

pîs - dirty; evil

porr (m.) - hair (on head, collective)

Q.

qehwe (f.) - coffee

qehweyî - brown

qelem (f.) - pen, pencil

qenc - good, well

qerar (f.) - decision

qeyser (m.) - caesar

qeza (f.) - accident

qîrîn, biqîre! - to scream

qiyamet (f.) - resurrection

qudret (f.) - power, strength

qurban (f.) - sacrifice

qul (f.) - hole

R.

rabûn (f.) - uprising, rebellion

rabên, rabe! - to stand up

rakirin, rabike - to lift up, to establish; to correct a (written) mistake

rast - true, right, straight, righteous

rastî (f.) - truth (bi rasti - truthfully)

rawestan, raweste! - to stand up, to stop

razan, raze! - sleep

reben - miserable, poor, unfortunate

reca kirin - to plead

reng (f.) - colour

rex (m.) - side; beside

reş - black

rê (f.) - road, way

rêç (f.) - footpath, track

rêvî (m.) -fox

rêz (f.) - line

rih (f.) - beard

rihat - comfortable

rihatî (f.) - rest, comfort

rind - goodness

ronahî (f.) - light, brightness

ronî - light, bright, clear

rovî (m.) - fox

rûnistin, rûne! - to sit

rûnistî - sitting

rûmet (f.) - honour, respect

S.

saket - lame

sal (f.) - year

sar - cold

sartir - colder

savar (f.) - bulgar (cracked wheat)

sed - one hundred

seh (m.) - dog

sekinîn, besekine! - to stop, to stand

ser - on, to

ser (m.) - head, chapter

serfirazî (f.) - triumph, victory

sê - three (when followed by a noun)

sêv (f.) - apple

sêzde - thirteen

sipe - white

sipehî - beautiful

sisê - three

sisêyan - third

siyah - black

sî - thirty

sor - red

sorik (f.) - measles

spehî - beautiful

spehîtî (f.) - beauty

Ş.

şabûn, şabibe! - to rejoice

şagirt (m.)- disciple

şah (m.) - king, ruler

şanzde - sixteen

şaşbûn, şaşbibe! - to be surprised; to be error

şaşıtî (f.) - surprise; error

şekir (m.) - sugar

şeş - six

şev (f.) - night

şewitandin, bişewitîne! - to burn (trans.)

şewitîn, bişewite! - to burn (intrans.)

şêr (m.) - lion

şêrîn - sweet

şêst - sixty

şêx (m.) - sheikh

şikeft (f.) - cave

şikir - thanks

şivan (m./f.) - shepherd

şiştin, bişo! - to wash

şiştî - washed

şîn - blue, blue-green, green

şîn dilbirîn - to go into mourning

şîn kirin - to grieve, to mourn

şîr (m.) - milk

şop (f.) - trail, trace

T.

ta - until, as far as

talan (f.) - plunder

taze - fresh, naked

te - you (sing.), yours

tebeq (f.) - level, class

tebîet - nature

temam - complete

tenê - except

teng - narrow, tight

tevlîhev - to be mixed up, tangled up

text (m.) - bed

textor (m.) - doctor

teze - see taze

têgihan - to arrive at, to understand

tijî kirin - to fill

tilih (f.) - finger

tim - always

tirb (f.) - grave

tirs (f.) - fear

tirsandin, bitirsîne! - to scare, to frighten

tirsîn, bitirse! - to be afraid

tişt (m.) - thing

tiştek - something, nothing (with neg. verb), anything

tifoîd - typhoid

toz (f.) - dust

tu - you (sing.)

tu - not any, none, nothing

tukes - nobody, no-one

tutişt - nothing

û.

û - and

V.

vebûn - to be opened

veşartin, veşêre! - to hide, to bury

vegerrin, vegerre! - to return

vekirin, veke! - to open

vexwarin, vexwe! - to drink

W.

walî (m./f.) - governor

wan - they, them, theirs

we - you (pl.), yours

wek - like, as

welidan, biwelide! - to give birth

wext (m.) - time

wextê ku - when

wey - woe

wê - she, her, hers

wilo ku - so... that...

wî - he, him, his

X.

xal (m.) - uncle (maternal)

xaltik (f.) - aunt (maternal)

xanî (m.) - house

xatir (f.) - favour

xebat (f.) - work

xeber (f.) - word

xelaskar (m.) - saviour

xelas kirin - to save

xem (f.) - sorrow

xew (f.) - sleep

xisitin, bixe! - to cause to fall, to throw, to put in

xort (m.) - youth

xortanî (f.) - youthfulness

xuh (f.) - sister

xwarin, bixwe! - to eat

xwarin (f.) - food

Xwedê (m.) - God

xwendegeh (f.) - school, university

xwendekar (m./f.) - student

xwendevan (m./f.) - scholar

xwendin, bixwêne / bixwêne! - to read

xwestin, bixwaze! - to want

xweş - pleasant, nice, fine, good

xweştir - better

xwîn (f.) - blood

Y.

ya - or

ya ... ya jî - either ... or...

yan - or

yanî - for example, in other words, meaning

yanzde - eleven

yek - one, somebody, someone

yekan - first

yekemîn - the very first

Z.

zanin, zanibe! - to know

zaro (m./f.) - child

zarok (m./f.) - child

zava (m.) - bridegroom, son-in-law, brother-in-law

zehf - very, too much

zengîn - rich

zer - yellow

zik (m.) - stomach

zilam (m.) - man, husband

zivistan (f.) - winter

zîv (m.) - silver

zîvî - silvery, made of silver

zor - difficult

zordan - to force

zû - quickly, easily

Made in the USA
San Bernardino, CA
02 February 2019